C-1441   CAREER EXAMINATION SERIES

This is your
PASSBOOK for...

Public Health Aide

Test Preparation Study Guide
Questions & Answers

COPYRIGHT NOTICE

This book is SOLELY intended for, is sold ONLY to, and its use is RESTRICTED to individual, bona fide applicants or candidates who qualify by virtue of having seriously filed applications for appropriate license, certificate, professional and/or promotional advancement, higher school matriculation, scholarship, or other legitimate requirements of education and/or governmental authorities.

This book is NOT intended for use, class instruction, tutoring, training, duplication, copying, reprinting, excerption, or adaptation, etc., by:

1) Other publishers
2) Proprietors and/or Instructors of "Coaching" and/or Preparatory Courses
3) Personnel and/or Training Divisions of commercial, industrial, and governmental organizations
4) Schools, colleges, or universities and/or their departments and staffs, including teachers and other personnel
5) Testing Agencies or Bureaus
6) Study groups which seek by the purchase of a single volume to copy and/or duplicate and/or adapt this material for use by the group as a whole without having purchased individual volumes for each of the members of the group
7) Et al.

Such persons would be in violation of appropriate Federal and State statutes.

PROVISION OF LICENSING AGREEMENTS – Recognized educational, commercial, industrial, and governmental institutions and organizations, and others legitimately engaged in educational pursuits, including training, testing, and measurement activities, may address request for a licensing agreement to the copyright owners, who will determine whether, and under what conditions, including fees and charges, the materials in this book may be used them. In other words, a licensing facility exists for the legitimate use of the material in this book on other than an individual basis. However, it is asseverated and affirmed here that the material in this book CANNOT be used without the receipt of the express permission of such a licensing agreement from the Publishers. Inquiries re licensing should be addressed to the company, attention rights and permissions department.

All rights reserved, including the right of reproduction in whole or in part, in any form or by any means, electronic or mechanical, including photocopying, recording, or by any information storage and retrieval system, without permission in writing from the Publisher.

Copyright © 2025 by
National Learning Corporation

212 Michael Drive, Syosset, NY 11791
(516) 921-8888 • www.passbooks.com
E-mail: info@passbooks.com

PASSBOOK® SERIES

THE *PASSBOOK® SERIES* has been created to prepare applicants and candidates for the ultimate academic battlefield – the examination room.

At some time in our lives, each and every one of us may be required to take an examination – for validation, matriculation, admission, qualification, registration, certification, or licensure.

Based on the assumption that every applicant or candidate has met the basic formal educational standards, has taken the required number of courses, and read the necessary texts, the *PASSBOOK® SERIES* furnishes the one special preparation which may assure passing with confidence, instead of failing with insecurity. Examination questions – together with answers – are furnished as the basic vehicle for study so that the mysteries of the examination and its compounding difficulties may be eliminated or diminished by a sure method.

This book is meant to help you pass your examination provided that you qualify and are serious in your objective.

The entire field is reviewed through the huge store of content information which is succinctly presented through a provocative and challenging approach – the question-and-answer method.

A climate of success is established by furnishing the correct answers at the end of each test.

You soon learn to recognize types of questions, forms of questions, and patterns of questioning. You may even begin to anticipate expected outcomes.

You perceive that many questions are repeated or adapted so that you can gain acute insights, which may enable you to score many sure points.

You learn how to confront new questions, or types of questions, and to attack them confidently and work out the correct answers.

You note objectives and emphases, and recognize pitfalls and dangers, so that you may make positive educational adjustments.

Moreover, you are kept fully informed in relation to new concepts, methods, practices, and directions in the field.

You discover that you are actually taking the examination all the time: you are preparing for the examination by "taking" an examination, not by reading extraneous and/or supererogatory textbooks.

In short, this PASSBOOK®, used directedly, should be an important factor in helping you to pass your test.

PUBLIC HEALTH AIDE

DUTIES
Assists medical personnel in the performance of paraprofessional duties in clinics; routes patients to examining rooms and assists them in dressing; holds children during examinations and treatment; weighs and measures patients; tests urine specimens; takes patients' temperatures and blood pressures; makes entries on patients' records. Assists in the physical set up of a clinic. Acts as clinic receptionist. Performs related work as required.

SCOPE OF THE EXAMINATION
The written test will be designed to test for knowledge, skills, and/or abilities in such areas as:
1. Assisting patients;
2. Clerical operations with letters and numbers; and
3. Alphabetizing.

HOW TO TAKE A TEST

I. YOU MUST PASS AN EXAMINATION

A. *WHAT EVERY CANDIDATE SHOULD KNOW*

Examination applicants often ask us for help in preparing for the written test. What can I study in advance? What kinds of questions will be asked? How will the test be given? How will the papers be graded?

As an applicant for a civil service examination, you may be wondering about some of these things. Our purpose here is to suggest effective methods of advance study and to describe civil service examinations.

Your chances for success on this examination can be increased if you know how to prepare. Those "pre-examination jitters" can be reduced if you know what to expect. You can even experience an adventure in good citizenship if you know why civil service exams are given.

B. *WHY ARE CIVIL SERVICE EXAMINATIONS GIVEN?*

Civil service examinations are important to you in two ways. As a citizen, you want public jobs filled by employees who know how to do their work. As a job seeker, you want a fair chance to compete for that job on an equal footing with other candidates. The best-known means of accomplishing this two-fold goal is the competitive examination.

Exams are widely publicized throughout the nation. They may be administered for jobs in federal, state, city, municipal, town or village governments or agencies.

Any citizen may apply, with some limitations, such as the age or residence of applicants. Your experience and education may be reviewed to see whether you meet the requirements for the particular examination. When these requirements exist, they are reasonable and applied consistently to all applicants. Thus, a competitive examination may cause you some uneasiness now, but it is your privilege and safeguard.

C. *HOW ARE CIVIL SERVICE EXAMS DEVELOPED?*

Examinations are carefully written by trained technicians who are specialists in the field known as "psychological measurement," in consultation with recognized authorities in the field of work that the test will cover. These experts recommend the subject matter areas or skills to be tested; only those knowledges or skills important to your success on the job are included. The most reliable books and source materials available are used as references. Together, the experts and technicians judge the difficulty level of the questions.

Test technicians know how to phrase questions so that the problem is clearly stated. Their ethics do not permit "trick" or "catch" questions. Questions may have been tried out on sample groups, or subjected to statistical analysis, to determine their usefulness.

Written tests are often used in combination with performance tests, ratings of training and experience, and oral interviews. All of these measures combine to form the best-known means of finding the right person for the right job.

II. HOW TO PASS THE WRITTEN TEST

A. NATURE OF THE EXAMINATION

To prepare intelligently for civil service examinations, you should know how they differ from school examinations you have taken. In school you were assigned certain definite pages to read or subjects to cover. The examination questions were quite detailed and usually emphasized memory. Civil service exams, on the other hand, try to discover your present ability to perform the duties of a position, plus your potentiality to learn these duties. In other words, a civil service exam attempts to predict how successful you will be. Questions cover such a broad area that they cannot be as minute and detailed as school exam questions.

In the public service similar kinds of work, or positions, are grouped together in one "class." This process is known as *position-classification*. All the positions in a class are paid according to the salary range for that class. One class title covers all of these positions, and they are all tested by the same examination.

B. FOUR BASIC STEPS

1) Study the announcement

How, then, can you know what subjects to study? Our best answer is: "Learn as much as possible about the class of positions for which you've applied." The exam will test the knowledge, skills and abilities needed to do the work.

Your most valuable source of information about the position you want is the official exam announcement. This announcement lists the training and experience qualifications. Check these standards and apply only if you come reasonably close to meeting them.

The brief description of the position in the examination announcement offers some clues to the subjects which will be tested. Think about the job itself. Review the duties in your mind. Can you perform them, or are there some in which you are rusty? Fill in the blank spots in your preparation.

Many jurisdictions preview the written test in the exam announcement by including a section called "Knowledge and Abilities Required," "Scope of the Examination," or some similar heading. Here you will find out specifically what fields will be tested.

2) Review your own background

Once you learn in general what the position is all about, and what you need to know to do the work, ask yourself which subjects you already know fairly well and which need improvement. You may wonder whether to concentrate on improving your strong areas or on building some background in your fields of weakness. When the announcement has specified "some knowledge" or "considerable knowledge," or has used adjectives like "beginning principles of..." or "advanced ... methods," you can get a clue as to the number and difficulty of questions to be asked in any given field. More questions, and hence broader coverage, would be included for those subjects which are more important in the work. Now weigh your strengths and weaknesses against the job requirements and prepare accordingly.

3) Determine the level of the position

Another way to tell how intensively you should prepare is to understand the level of the job for which you are applying. Is it the entering level? In other words, is this the position in which beginners in a field of work are hired? Or is it an intermediate or advanced level? Sometimes this is indicated by such words as "Junior" or "Senior" in the class title. Other jurisdictions use Roman numerals to designate the level – Clerk I, Clerk II, for example. The word "Supervisor" sometimes appears in the title. If the level is not indicated by the title, check the description of duties. Will you be working under very close supervision, or will you have responsibility for independent decisions in this work?

4) Choose appropriate study materials

Now that you know the subjects to be examined and the relative amount of each subject to be covered, you can choose suitable study materials. For beginning level jobs, or even advanced ones, if you have a pronounced weakness in some aspect of your training, read a modern, standard textbook in that field. Be sure it is up to date and has general coverage. Such books are normally available at your library, and the librarian will be glad to help you locate one. For entry-level positions, questions of appropriate difficulty are chosen – neither highly advanced questions, nor those too simple. Such questions require careful thought but not advanced training.

If the position for which you are applying is technical or advanced, you will read more advanced, specialized material. If you are already familiar with the basic principles of your field, elementary textbooks would waste your time. Concentrate on advanced textbooks and technical periodicals. Think through the concepts and review difficult problems in your field.

These are all general sources. You can get more ideas on your own initiative, following these leads. For example, training manuals and publications of the government agency which employs workers in your field can be useful, particularly for technical and professional positions. A letter or visit to the government department involved may result in more specific study suggestions, and certainly will provide you with a more definite idea of the exact nature of the position you are seeking.

III. KINDS OF TESTS

Tests are used for purposes other than measuring knowledge and ability to perform specified duties. For some positions, it is equally important to test ability to make adjustments to new situations or to profit from training. In others, basic mental abilities not dependent on information are essential. Questions which test these things may not appear as pertinent to the duties of the position as those which test for knowledge and information. Yet they are often highly important parts of a fair examination. For very general questions, it is almost impossible to help you direct your study efforts. What we can do is to point out some of the more common of these general abilities needed in public service positions and describe some typical questions.

1) General information

Broad, general information has been found useful for predicting job success in some kinds of work. This is tested in a variety of ways, from vocabulary lists to questions about current events. Basic background in some field of work, such as sociology or economics, may be sampled in a group of questions. Often these are principles which have become familiar to most persons through exposure rather than through formal training. It is difficult to advise you how to study for these questions; being alert to the world around you is our best suggestion.

2) Verbal ability

An example of an ability needed in many positions is verbal or language ability. Verbal ability is, in brief, the ability to use and understand words. Vocabulary and grammar tests are typical measures of this ability. Reading comprehension or paragraph interpretation questions are common in many kinds of civil service tests. You are given a paragraph of written material and asked to find its central meaning.

3) Numerical ability

Number skills can be tested by the familiar arithmetic problem, by checking paired lists of numbers to see which are alike and which are different, or by interpreting charts and graphs. In the latter test, a graph may be printed in the test booklet which you are asked to use as the basis for answering questions.

4) Observation

A popular test for law-enforcement positions is the observation test. A picture is shown to you for several minutes, then taken away. Questions about the picture test your ability to observe both details and larger elements.

5) Following directions

In many positions in the public service, the employee must be able to carry out written instructions dependably and accurately. You may be given a chart with several columns, each column listing a variety of information. The questions require you to carry out directions involving the information given in the chart.

6) Skills and aptitudes

Performance tests effectively measure some manual skills and aptitudes. When the skill is one in which you are trained, such as typing or shorthand, you can practice. These tests are often very much like those given in business school or high school courses. For many of the other skills and aptitudes, however, no short-time preparation can be made. Skills and abilities natural to you or that you have developed throughout your lifetime are being tested.

Many of the general questions just described provide all the data needed to answer the questions and ask you to use your reasoning ability to find the answers. Your best preparation for these tests, as well as for tests of facts and ideas, is to be at your physical and mental best. You, no doubt, have your own methods of getting into an exam-taking mood and keeping "in shape." The next section lists some ideas on this subject.

IV. KINDS OF QUESTIONS

Only rarely is the "essay" question, which you answer in narrative form, used in civil service tests. Civil service tests are usually of the short-answer type. Full instructions for answering these questions will be given to you at the examination. But in case this is your first experience with short-answer questions and separate answer sheets, here is what you need to know:

1) Multiple-choice Questions

Most popular of the short-answer questions is the "multiple choice" or "best answer" question. It can be used, for example, to test for factual knowledge, ability to solve problems or judgment in meeting situations found at work.

A multiple-choice question is normally one of three types—
- It can begin with an incomplete statement followed by several possible endings. You are to find the one ending which *best* completes the statement, although some of the others may not be entirely wrong.
- It can also be a complete statement in the form of a question which is answered by choosing one of the statements listed.

- It can be in the form of a problem – again you select the best answer.

Here is an example of a multiple-choice question with a discussion which should give you some clues as to the method for choosing the right answer:

When an employee has a complaint about his assignment, the action which will *best* help him overcome his difficulty is to
   A. discuss his difficulty with his coworkers
   B. take the problem to the head of the organization
   C. take the problem to the person who gave him the assignment
   D. say nothing to anyone about his complaint

In answering this question, you should study each of the choices to find which is best. Consider choice "A" – Certainly an employee may discuss his complaint with fellow employees, but no change or improvement can result, and the complaint remains unresolved. Choice "B" is a poor choice since the head of the organization probably does not know what assignment you have been given, and taking your problem to him is known as "going over the head" of the supervisor. The supervisor, or person who made the assignment, is the person who can clarify it or correct any injustice. Choice "C" is, therefore, correct. To say nothing, as in choice "D," is unwise. Supervisors have and interest in knowing the problems employees are facing, and the employee is seeking a solution to his problem.

2) True/False Questions

The "true/false" or "right/wrong" form of question is sometimes used. Here a complete statement is given. Your job is to decide whether the statement is right or wrong.

SAMPLE: A roaming cell-phone call to a nearby city costs less than a non-roaming call to a distant city.

This statement is wrong, or false, since roaming calls are more expensive.

This is not a complete list of all possible question forms, although most of the others are variations of these common types. You will always get complete directions for answering questions. Be sure you understand *how* to mark your answers – ask questions until you do.

V. RECORDING YOUR ANSWERS

Computer terminals are used more and more today for many different kinds of exams.

For an examination with very few applicants, you may be told to record your answers in the test booklet itself. Separate answer sheets are much more common. If this separate answer sheet is to be scored by machine – and this is often the case – it is highly important that you mark your answers correctly in order to get credit.

An electronic scoring machine is often used in civil service offices because of the speed with which papers can be scored. Machine-scored answer sheets must be marked with a pencil, which will be given to you. This pencil has a high graphite content which responds to the electronic scoring machine. As a matter of fact, stray dots may register as answers, so do not let your pencil rest on the answer sheet while you are pondering the correct answer. Also, if your pencil lead breaks or is otherwise defective, ask for another.

Since the answer sheet will be dropped in a slot in the scoring machine, be careful not to bend the corners or get the paper crumpled.

The answer sheet normally has five vertical columns of numbers, with 30 numbers to a column. These numbers correspond to the question numbers in your test booklet. After each number, going across the page are four or five pairs of dotted lines. These short dotted lines have small letters or numbers above them. The first two pairs may also have a "T" or "F" above the letters. This indicates that the first two pairs only are to be used if the questions are of the true-false type. If the questions are multiple choice, disregard the "T" and "F" and pay attention only to the small letters or numbers.

Answer your questions in the manner of the sample that follows:

32. The largest city in the United States is
    A. Washington, D.C.
    B. New York City
    C. Chicago
    D. Detroit
    E. San Francisco

1) Choose the answer you think is best. (New York City is the largest, so "B" is correct.)
2) Find the row of dotted lines numbered the same as the question you are answering. (Find row number 32)
3) Find the pair of dotted lines corresponding to the answer. (Find the pair of lines under the mark "B.")
4) Make a solid black mark between the dotted lines.

VI. BEFORE THE TEST

Common sense will help you find procedures to follow to get ready for an examination. Too many of us, however, overlook these sensible measures. Indeed, nervousness and fatigue have been found to be the most serious reasons why applicants fail to do their best on civil service tests. Here is a list of reminders:

- Begin your preparation early – Don't wait until the last minute to go scurrying around for books and materials or to find out what the position is all about.
- Prepare continuously – An hour a night for a week is better than an all-night cram session. This has been definitely established. What is more, a night a week for a month will return better dividends than crowding your study into a shorter period of time.
- Locate the place of the exam – You have been sent a notice telling you when and where to report for the examination. If the location is in a different town or otherwise unfamiliar to you, it would be well to inquire the best route and learn something about the building.
- Relax the night before the test – Allow your mind to rest. Do not study at all that night. Plan some mild recreation or diversion; then go to bed early and get a good night's sleep.
- Get up early enough to make a leisurely trip to the place for the test – This way unforeseen events, traffic snarls, unfamiliar buildings, etc. will not upset you.
- Dress comfortably – A written test is not a fashion show. You will be known by number and not by name, so wear something comfortable.

- Leave excess paraphernalia at home – Shopping bags and odd bundles will get in your way. You need bring only the items mentioned in the official notice you received; usually everything you need is provided. Do not bring reference books to the exam. They will only confuse those last minutes and be taken away from you when in the test room.
- Arrive somewhat ahead of time – If because of transportation schedules you must get there very early, bring a newspaper or magazine to take your mind off yourself while waiting.
- Locate the examination room – When you have found the proper room, you will be directed to the seat or part of the room where you will sit. Sometimes you are given a sheet of instructions to read while you are waiting. Do not fill out any forms until you are told to do so; just read them and be prepared.
- Relax and prepare to listen to the instructions
- If you have any physical problem that may keep you from doing your best, be sure to tell the test administrator. If you are sick or in poor health, you really cannot do your best on the exam. You can come back and take the test some other time.

VII. AT THE TEST

The day of the test is here and you have the test booklet in your hand. The temptation to get going is very strong. Caution! There is more to success than knowing the right answers. You must know how to identify your papers and understand variations in the type of short-answer question used in this particular examination. Follow these suggestions for maximum results from your efforts:

1) Cooperate with the monitor

The test administrator has a duty to create a situation in which you can be as much at ease as possible. He will give instructions, tell you when to begin, check to see that you are marking your answer sheet correctly, and so on. He is not there to guard you, although he will see that your competitors do not take unfair advantage. He wants to help you do your best.

2) Listen to all instructions

Don't jump the gun! Wait until you understand all directions. In most civil service tests you get more time than you need to answer the questions. So don't be in a hurry. Read each word of instructions until you clearly understand the meaning. Study the examples, listen to all announcements and follow directions. Ask questions if you do not understand what to do.

3) Identify your papers

Civil service exams are usually identified by number only. You will be assigned a number; you must not put your name on your test papers. Be sure to copy your number correctly. Since more than one exam may be given, copy your exact examination title.

4) Plan your time

Unless you are told that a test is a "speed" or "rate of work" test, speed itself is usually not important. Time enough to answer all the questions will be provided, but this does not mean that you have all day. An overall time limit has been set. Divide the total time (in minutes) by the number of questions to determine the approximate time you have for each question.

5) Do not linger over difficult questions

If you come across a difficult question, mark it with a paper clip (useful to have along) and come back to it when you have been through the booklet. One caution if you do this – be sure to skip a number on your answer sheet as well. Check often to be sure that you have not lost your place and that you are marking in the row numbered the same as the question you are answering.

6) Read the questions

Be sure you know what the question asks! Many capable people are unsuccessful because they failed to *read* the questions correctly.

7) Answer all questions

Unless you have been instructed that a penalty will be deducted for incorrect answers, it is better to guess than to omit a question.

8) Speed tests

It is often better NOT to guess on speed tests. It has been found that on timed tests people are tempted to spend the last few seconds before time is called in marking answers at random – without even reading them – in the hope of picking up a few extra points. To discourage this practice, the instructions may warn you that your score will be "corrected" for guessing. That is, a penalty will be applied. The incorrect answers will be deducted from the correct ones, or some other penalty formula will be used.

9) Review your answers

If you finish before time is called, go back to the questions you guessed or omitted to give them further thought. Review other answers if you have time.

10) Return your test materials

If you are ready to leave before others have finished or time is called, take ALL your materials to the monitor and leave quietly. Never take any test material with you. The monitor can discover whose papers are not complete, and taking a test booklet may be grounds for disqualification.

VIII. EXAMINATION TECHNIQUES

1) Read the general instructions carefully. These are usually printed on the first page of the exam booklet. As a rule, these instructions refer to the timing of the examination; the fact that you should not start work until the signal and must stop work at a signal, etc. If there are any *special* instructions, such as a choice of questions to be answered, make sure that you note this instruction carefully.

2) When you are ready to start work on the examination, that is as soon as the signal has been given, read the instructions to each question booklet, underline any key words or phrases, such as *least, best, outline, describe* and the like. In this way you will tend to answer as requested rather than discover on reviewing your paper that you *listed without describing*, that you selected the *worst* choice rather than the *best* choice, etc.

3) If the examination is of the objective or multiple-choice type – that is, each question will also give a series of possible answers: A, B, C or D, and you are called upon to select the best answer and write the letter next to that answer on your answer paper – it is advisable to start answering each question in turn. There may be anywhere from 50 to 100 such questions in the three or four hours allotted and you can see how much time would be taken if you read through all the questions before beginning to answer any. Furthermore, if you come across a question or group of questions which you know would be difficult to answer, it would undoubtedly affect your handling of all the other questions.

4) If the examination is of the essay type and contains but a few questions, it is a moot point as to whether you should read all the questions before starting to answer any one. Of course, if you are given a choice – say five out of seven and the like – then it is essential to read all the questions so you can eliminate the two that are most difficult. If, however, you are asked to answer all the questions, there may be danger in trying to answer the easiest one first because you may find that you will spend too much time on it. The best technique is to answer the first question, then proceed to the second, etc.

5) Time your answers. Before the exam begins, write down the time it started, then add the time allowed for the examination and write down the time it must be completed, then divide the time available somewhat as follows:
    - If 3-1/2 hours are allowed, that would be 210 minutes. If you have 80 objective-type questions, that would be an average of 2-1/2 minutes per question. Allow yourself no more than 2 minutes per question, or a total of 160 minutes, which will permit about 50 minutes to review.
    - If for the time allotment of 210 minutes there are 7 essay questions to answer, that would average about 30 minutes a question. Give yourself only 25 minutes per question so that you have about 35 minutes to review.

6) The most important instruction is to *read each question* and make sure you know what is wanted. The second most important instruction is to *time yourself properly* so that you answer every question. The third most important instruction is to *answer every question*. Guess if you have to but include something for each question. Remember that you will receive no credit for a blank and will probably receive some credit if you write something in answer to an essay question. If you guess a letter – say "B" for a multiple-choice question – you may have guessed right. If you leave a blank as an answer to a multiple-choice question, the examiners may respect your feelings but it will not add a point to your score. Some exams may penalize you for wrong answers, so in such cases *only*, you may not want to guess unless you have some basis for your answer.

7) Suggestions
    a. Objective-type questions
        1. Examine the question booklet for proper sequence of pages and questions
        2. Read all instructions carefully
        3. Skip any question which seems too difficult; return to it after all other questions have been answered
        4. Apportion your time properly; do not spend too much time on any single question or group of questions

5. Note and underline key words – *all, most, fewest, least, best, worst, same, opposite,* etc.
6. Pay particular attention to negatives
7. Note unusual option, e.g., unduly long, short, complex, different or similar in content to the body of the question
8. Observe the use of "hedging" words – *probably, may, most likely,* etc.
9. Make sure that your answer is put next to the same number as the question
10. Do not second-guess unless you have good reason to believe the second answer is definitely more correct
11. Cross out original answer if you decide another answer is more accurate; do not erase until you are ready to hand your paper in
12. Answer all questions; guess unless instructed otherwise
13. Leave time for review

   b. Essay questions
1. Read each question carefully
2. Determine exactly what is wanted. Underline key words or phrases.
3. Decide on outline or paragraph answer
4. Include many different points and elements unless asked to develop any one or two points or elements
5. Show impartiality by giving pros and cons unless directed to select one side only
6. Make and write down any assumptions you find necessary to answer the questions
7. Watch your English, grammar, punctuation and choice of words
8. Time your answers; don't crowd material

8) Answering the essay question

Most essay questions can be answered by framing the specific response around several key words or ideas. Here are a few such key words or ideas:

M's: manpower, materials, methods, money, management
P's: purpose, program, policy, plan, procedure, practice, problems, pitfalls, personnel, public relations

   a. Six basic steps in handling problems:
1. Preliminary plan and background development
2. Collect information, data and facts
3. Analyze and interpret information, data and facts
4. Analyze and develop solutions as well as make recommendations
5. Prepare report and sell recommendations
6. Install recommendations and follow up effectiveness

   b. Pitfalls to avoid
1. *Taking things for granted* – A statement of the situation does not necessarily imply that each of the elements is necessarily true; for example, a complaint may be invalid and biased so that all that can be taken for granted is that a complaint has been registered

2. *Considering only one side of a situation* – Wherever possible, indicate several alternatives and then point out the reasons you selected the best one
3. *Failing to indicate follow up* – Whenever your answer indicates action on your part, make certain that you will take proper follow-up action to see how successful your recommendations, procedures or actions turn out to be
4. *Taking too long in answering any single question* – Remember to time your answers properly

IX. AFTER THE TEST

Scoring procedures differ in detail among civil service jurisdictions although the general principles are the same. Whether the papers are hand-scored or graded by machine we have described, they are nearly always graded by number. That is, the person who marks the paper knows only the number – never the name – of the applicant. Not until all the papers have been graded will they be matched with names. If other tests, such as training and experience or oral interview ratings have been given, scores will be combined. Different parts of the examination usually have different weights. For example, the written test might count 60 percent of the final grade, and a rating of training and experience 40 percent. In many jurisdictions, veterans will have a certain number of points added to their grades.

After the final grade has been determined, the names are placed in grade order and an eligible list is established. There are various methods for resolving ties between those who get the same final grade – probably the most common is to place first the name of the person whose application was received first. Job offers are made from the eligible list in the order the names appear on it. You will be notified of your grade and your rank as soon as all these computations have been made. This will be done as rapidly as possible.

People who are found to meet the requirements in the announcement are called "eligibles." Their names are put on a list of eligible candidates. An eligible's chances of getting a job depend on how high he stands on this list and how fast agencies are filling jobs from the list.

When a job is to be filled from a list of eligibles, the agency asks for the names of people on the list of eligibles for that job. When the civil service commission receives this request, it sends to the agency the names of the three people highest on this list. Or, if the job to be filled has specialized requirements, the office sends the agency the names of the top three persons who meet these requirements from the general list.

The appointing officer makes a choice from among the three people whose names were sent to him. If the selected person accepts the appointment, the names of the others are put back on the list to be considered for future openings.

That is the rule in hiring from all kinds of eligible lists, whether they are for typist, carpenter, chemist, or something else. For every vacancy, the appointing officer has his choice of any one of the top three eligibles on the list. This explains why the person whose name is on top of the list sometimes does not get an appointment when some of the persons lower on the list do. If the appointing officer chooses the second or third eligible, the No. 1 eligible does not get a job at once, but stays on the list until he is appointed or the list is terminated.

X. HOW TO PASS THE INTERVIEW TEST

The examination for which you applied requires an oral interview test. You have already taken the written test and you are now being called for the interview test – the final part of the formal examination.

You may think that it is not possible to prepare for an interview test and that there are no procedures to follow during an interview. Our purpose is to point out some things you can do in advance that will help you and some good rules to follow and pitfalls to avoid while you are being interviewed.

What is an interview supposed to test?

The written examination is designed to test the technical knowledge and competence of the candidate; the oral is designed to evaluate intangible qualities, not readily measured otherwise, and to establish a list showing the relative fitness of each candidate – as measured against his competitors – for the position sought. Scoring is not on the basis of "right" and "wrong," but on a sliding scale of values ranging from "not passable" to "outstanding." As a matter of fact, it is possible to achieve a relatively low score without a single "incorrect" answer because of evident weakness in the qualities being measured.

Occasionally, an examination may consist entirely of an oral test – either an individual or a group oral. In such cases, information is sought concerning the technical knowledges and abilities of the candidate, since there has been no written examination for this purpose. More commonly, however, an oral test is used to supplement a written examination.

Who conducts interviews?

The composition of oral boards varies among different jurisdictions. In nearly all, a representative of the personnel department serves as chairman. One of the members of the board may be a representative of the department in which the candidate would work. In some cases, "outside experts" are used, and, frequently, a businessman or some other representative of the general public is asked to serve. Labor and management or other special groups may be represented. The aim is to secure the services of experts in the appropriate field.

However the board is composed, it is a good idea (and not at all improper or unethical) to ascertain in advance of the interview who the members are and what groups they represent. When you are introduced to them, you will have some idea of their backgrounds and interests, and at least you will not stutter and stammer over their names.

What should be done before the interview?

While knowledge about the board members is useful and takes some of the surprise element out of the interview, there is other preparation which is more substantive. It *is* possible to prepare for an oral interview – in several ways:

1) Keep a copy of your application and review it carefully before the interview

This may be the only document before the oral board, and the starting point of the interview. Know what education and experience you have listed there, and the sequence and dates of all of it. Sometimes the board will ask you to review the highlights of your experience for them; you should not have to hem and haw doing it.

2) Study the class specification and the examination announcement

Usually, the oral board has one or both of these to guide them. The qualities, characteristics or knowledges required by the position sought are stated in these documents. They offer valuable clues as to the nature of the oral interview. For example, if the job involves supervisory responsibilities, the announcement will usually indicate that knowledge of modern supervisory methods and the qualifications of the candidate as a supervisor will be tested. If so, you can expect such questions, frequently in the form of a hypothetical situation which you are expected to solve. NEVER go into an oral without knowledge of the duties and responsibilities of the job you seek.

3) Think through each qualification required
Try to visualize the kind of questions you would ask if you were a board member. How well could you answer them? Try especially to appraise your own knowledge and background in each area, *measured against the job sought*, and identify any areas in which you are weak. Be critical and realistic – do not flatter yourself.

4) Do some general reading in areas in which you feel you may be weak
For example, if the job involves supervision and your past experience has NOT, some general reading in supervisory methods and practices, particularly in the field of human relations, might be useful. Do NOT study agency procedures or detailed manuals. The oral board will be testing your understanding and capacity, not your memory.

5) Get a good night's sleep and watch your general health and mental attitude
You will want a clear head at the interview. Take care of a cold or any other minor ailment, and of course, no hangovers.

What should be done on the day of the interview?
Now comes the day of the interview itself. Give yourself plenty of time to get there. Plan to arrive somewhat ahead of the scheduled time, particularly if your appointment is in the fore part of the day. If a previous candidate fails to appear, the board might be ready for you a bit early. By early afternoon an oral board is almost invariably behind schedule if there are many candidates, and you may have to wait. Take along a book or magazine to read, or your application to review, but leave any extraneous material in the waiting room when you go in for your interview. In any event, relax and compose yourself.

The matter of dress is important. The board is forming impressions about you – from your experience, your manners, your attitude, and your appearance. Give your personal appearance careful attention. Dress your best, but not your flashiest. Choose conservative, appropriate clothing, and be sure it is immaculate. This is a business interview, and your appearance should indicate that you regard it as such. Besides, being well groomed and properly dressed will help boost your confidence.

Sooner or later, someone will call your name and escort you into the interview room. *This is it*. From here on you are on your own. It is too late for any more preparation. But remember, you asked for this opportunity to prove your fitness, and you are here because your request was granted.

What happens when you go in?
The usual sequence of events will be as follows: The clerk (who is often the board stenographer) will introduce you to the chairman of the oral board, who will introduce you to the other members of the board. Acknowledge the introductions before you sit down. Do not be surprised if you find a microphone facing you or a stenotypist sitting by. Oral interviews are usually recorded in the event of an appeal or other review.

Usually the chairman of the board will open the interview by reviewing the highlights of your education and work experience from your application – primarily for the benefit of the other members of the board, as well as to get the material into the record. Do not interrupt or comment unless there is an error or significant misinterpretation; if that is the case, do not hesitate. But do not quibble about insignificant matters. Also, he will usually ask you some question about your education, experience or your present job – partly to get you to start talking and to establish the interviewing "rapport." He may start the actual questioning, or turn it over to one of the other members. Frequently, each member undertakes the questioning on a particular area, one in which he is perhaps most competent, so you can expect each member to participate in the examination. Because time is limited, you may also expect some rather abrupt switches in the direction the questioning takes, so do not be upset by it. Normally, a board member will not pursue a single line of questioning unless he discovers a particular strength or weakness.

After each member has participated, the chairman will usually ask whether any member has any further questions, then will ask you if you have anything you wish to add. Unless you are expecting this question, it may floor you. Worse, it may start you off on an extended, extemporaneous speech. The board is not usually seeking more information. The question is principally to offer you a last opportunity to present further qualifications or to indicate that you have nothing to add. So, if you feel that a significant qualification or characteristic has been overlooked, it is proper to point it out in a sentence or so. Do not compliment the board on the thoroughness of their examination – they have been sketchy, and you know it. If you wish, merely say, "No thank you, I have nothing further to add." This is a point where you can "talk yourself out" of a good impression or fail to present an important bit of information. Remember, *you close the interview yourself*.

The chairman will then say, "That is all, Mr. _____, thank you." Do not be startled; the interview is over, and quicker than you think. Thank him, gather your belongings and take your leave. Save your sigh of relief for the other side of the door.

How to put your best foot forward

Throughout this entire process, you may feel that the board individually and collectively is trying to pierce your defenses, seek out your hidden weaknesses and embarrass and confuse you. Actually, this is not true. They are obliged to make an appraisal of your qualifications for the job you are seeking, and they want to see you in your best light. Remember, they must interview all candidates and a non-cooperative candidate may become a failure in spite of their best efforts to bring out his qualifications. Here are 15 suggestions that will help you:

1) Be natural – Keep your attitude confident, not cocky

If you are not confident that you can do the job, do not expect the board to be. Do not apologize for your weaknesses, try to bring out your strong points. The board is interested in a positive, not negative, presentation. Cockiness will antagonize any board member and make him wonder if you are covering up a weakness by a false show of strength.

2) Get comfortable, but don't lounge or sprawl

Sit erectly but not stiffly. A careless posture may lead the board to conclude that you are careless in other things, or at least that you are not impressed by the importance of the occasion. Either conclusion is natural, even if incorrect. Do not fuss with your clothing, a pencil or an ashtray. Your hands may occasionally be useful to emphasize a point; do not let them become a point of distraction.

3) Do not wisecrack or make small talk

This is a serious situation, and your attitude should show that you consider it as such. Further, the time of the board is limited – they do not want to waste it, and neither should you.

4) Do not exaggerate your experience or abilities

In the first place, from information in the application or other interviews and sources, the board may know more about you than you think. Secondly, you probably will not get away with it. An experienced board is rather adept at spotting such a situation, so do not take the chance.

5) If you know a board member, do not make a point of it, yet do not hide it

Certainly you are not fooling him, and probably not the other members of the board. Do not try to take advantage of your acquaintanceship – it will probably do you little good.

6) Do not dominate the interview

Let the board do that. They will give you the clues – do not assume that you have to do all the talking. Realize that the board has a number of questions to ask you, and do not try to take up all the interview time by showing off your extensive knowledge of the answer to the first one.

7) Be attentive

You only have 20 minutes or so, and you should keep your attention at its sharpest throughout. When a member is addressing a problem or question to you, give him your undivided attention. Address your reply principally to him, but do not exclude the other board members.

8) Do not interrupt

A board member may be stating a problem for you to analyze. He will ask you a question when the time comes. Let him state the problem, and wait for the question.

9) Make sure you understand the question

Do not try to answer until you are sure what the question is. If it is not clear, restate it in your own words or ask the board member to clarify it for you. However, do not haggle about minor elements.

10) Reply promptly but not hastily

A common entry on oral board rating sheets is "candidate responded readily," or "candidate hesitated in replies." Respond as promptly and quickly as you can, but do not jump to a hasty, ill-considered answer.

11) Do not be peremptory in your answers

A brief answer is proper – but do not fire your answer back. That is a losing game from your point of view. The board member can probably ask questions much faster than you can answer them.

12) Do not try to create the answer you think the board member wants

He is interested in what kind of mind you have and how it works – not in playing games. Furthermore, he can usually spot this practice and will actually grade you down on it.

13) Do not switch sides in your reply merely to agree with a board member

Frequently, a member will take a contrary position merely to draw you out and to see if you are willing and able to defend your point of view. Do not start a debate, yet do not surrender a good position. If a position is worth taking, it is worth defending.

14) Do not be afraid to admit an error in judgment if you are shown to be wrong
The board knows that you are forced to reply without any opportunity for careful consideration. Your answer may be demonstrably wrong. If so, admit it and get on with the interview.

15) Do not dwell at length on your present job
The opening question may relate to your present assignment. Answer the question but do not go into an extended discussion. You are being examined for a *new* job, not your present one. As a matter of fact, try to phrase ALL your answers in terms of the job for which you are being examined.

Basis of Rating
Probably you will forget most of these "do's" and "don'ts" when you walk into the oral interview room. Even remembering them all will not ensure you a passing grade. Perhaps you did not have the qualifications in the first place. But remembering them will help you to put your best foot forward, without treading on the toes of the board members.

Rumor and popular opinion to the contrary notwithstanding, an oral board wants you to make the best appearance possible. They know you are under pressure – but they also want to see how you respond to it as a guide to what your reaction would be under the pressures of the job you seek. They will be influenced by the degree of poise you display, the personal traits you show and the manner in which you respond.

ABOUT THIS BOOK

This book contains tests divided into Examination Sections. Go through each test, answering every question in the margin. We have also attached a sample answer sheet at the back of the book that can be removed and used. At the end of each test look at the answer key and check your answers. On the ones you got wrong, look at the right answer choice and learn. Do not fill in the answers first. Do not memorize the questions and answers, but understand the answer and principles involved. On your test, the questions will likely be different from the samples. Questions are changed and new ones added. If you understand these past questions you should have success with any changes that arise. Tests may consist of several types of questions. We have additional books on each subject should more study be advisable or necessary for you. Finally, the more you study, the better prepared you will be. This book is intended to be the last thing you study before you walk into the examination room. Prior study of relevant texts is also recommended. NLC publishes some of these in our Fundamental Series. Knowledge and good sense are important factors in passing your exam. Good luck also helps. So now study this Passbook, absorb the material contained within and take that knowledge into the examination. Then do your best to pass that exam.

EXAMINATION SECTION

EXAMINATION SECTION
TEST 1

DIRECTIONS: Each question or incomplete statement is followed by several suggested answers or completions. Select the one that BEST answers the question or completes the statement. *PRINT THE LETTER OF THE CORRECT ANSWER IN THE SPACE AT THE RIGHT.*

1. Assume that you are assigned to a health center. A middle-aged man walks in and says that he doesn't feel well. He complains of a slight pain in the chest and has difficulty breathing.
Of the following actions, the one you should take is to

   A. isolate him immediately as he may have *Asian flu*
   B. find out what he has eaten as he may have food poisoning
   C. ask him to sit down and see if he can catch his breath
   D. see that he is seated and then call a doctor

1.____

2. A baby who has been brought to the health center for an examination has been crying continuously for 20 minutes. The BEST of the following actions you should take is to

   A. have the baby examined by the first available physician
   B. ask the others who are waiting if they would object to the baby being examined out of turn
   C. call the situation to the attention of the nurse in charge
   D. do nothing as there are probably others who are ill and need to see the doctor

2.____

3. Suppose that a mother comes into the health center, carrying a 3-year-old child who is ill. The mother tells you that the child has a temperature of 102°F, his nose is stuffed, and he is sneezing.
For you to seat the mother and child apart from the others who are waiting for the physician is

   A. *correct;* the other children and adults in the clinic should not be exposed to a disease which may be contagious
   B. *incorrect;* the mother might be offended if she were treated differently than the other patients
   C. *correct;* the nurse is in a good position to diagnose patients when the doctor is not available
   D. *incorrect;* you should wait until the physician makes his diagnosis before isolating the child

3.____

4. In the performance of her work, it is not enough that the employee be alert to the immediate demands of her own job; she must be constantly aware of the basic function of the clinic.
This statement means that a worker should view the ultimate purpose of her job as

   A. giving effective service to patients
   B. getting the most work done in the shortest time
   C. following to the letter all orders given to her
   D. reporting punctually and working diligently

4.____

5. While serving at an eye clinic, you are instructed to answer the phone by saying, *Eye Clinic, Miss Jones speaking.*
   Of the following, the BEST reason for this practice is that

   A. it sets the tone for a brief, concise telephone conversation
   B. it is the standard practice recommended by the telephone company and is familiar to callers
   C. the caller will understand that he cannot ask for medical information, since you are not a physician
   D. the caller will know whether he is speaking to the person he wants to reach

6. If a telephone call is received for a doctor while he is examining a patient, it would be BEST to

   A. tell the caller to telephone again when the doctor can receive a call
   B. take the caller's telephone number and have the doctor return the call when he is free
   C. ask the nature of the call in order to determine if it requires the doctor's immediate attention
   D. refer the call to the nurse in charge as she may have the information the caller requires

7. Suppose that a patient who attends the clinic has made frequent complaints, usually unjustified.
   Of the following, the BEST reason for not ignoring another complaint from her is that

   A. she is likely to take her complaint to a higher level
   B. even though past complaints have been unjustified, this particular one may require attention
   C. a patient is often pacified if you pretend that you will look into her complaint
   D. no distinction should be made in your attitude toward patients

8. Clinic appointments are less likely to be broken if you

   A. make appointments on dates which are convenient for the patients
   B. stress to each patient that a broken appointment inconveniences other patients
   C. threaten not to make any more appointments for patients who break appointments without a good reason
   D. arrange the schedule of appointments so that patients do not have to wait in the clinic

9. Assume that every day the schedule of the clinic is severely disrupted because several patients without appointments must be treated for emergency conditions. Of the following, the BEST suggestion you could make in order to minimize disruption is that

   A. one morning a week be set aside when all emergency cases will be treated
   B. applicants who claim emergency conditions be screened to see which of them really need emergency treatment
   C. unassigned periods be allowed in the schedule in anticipation of emergency cases
   D. the clinic be kept open each evening until all patients have been treated

10. Suppose that a woman who is scheduled to appear at 3:30 P.M. comes into the clinic at 10 A.M. and says she is ill and must see the doctor at once. The clinic is already quite crowded.
    It would be BEST for you to

    A. try to determine if she is really ill, since some patients use the claim as a ruse to get prompt attention
    B. tell her to return at the proper time, since the other patients will become disorderly if others are taken before they are
    C. see if the head nurse will take her out of turn, since she may need prompt care
    D. see if a clinic physician is willing to see her, since public reaction would be hostile if the condition of the woman became worse while waiting

11. Some authorities advocate that the mother not stay in the same room when a child of 3 or 4 is being treated by the doctor.
    Of the following, the BEST reason for this is that the

    A. mother might become upset if she watches the treatment
    B. child is less likely to accept the doctor's authority
    C. mother will prolong the examination by questioning the doctor about her child
    D. child will mature more rapidly if he is not always accompanied by his mother

12. Assume that a patient tells you that he is not going to follow the treatment recommended by the physician because he doesn't have long to live anyway.
    It would be BEST for you to

    A. report the conversation to the physician
    B. point out to the patient that it is foolish to come for treatment if he will not follow the recommendations given him by the physician
    C. explain to the patient that he will live longer and less painfully if he follows the physician's recommendations
    D. try to get a relative in whom the patient has confidence to persuade him to follow the physician's recommendations

13. Suppose that a patient who has just received treatment in the clinic complains loudly that she was kept waiting a lone time and then received hasty and inadequate treatment.
    It is BEST for you to

    A. explain that treatment is necessarily hasty because the clinic is busy
    B. avoid arguing with her, since ill people are often overwrought
    C. tell her she is not qualified to decide whether treatment is adequate
    D. refer the patient back to the physician for completion of treatment

14. Assume that a patient who has been coming to the clinic for some time asks you, *Do I have a heart condition?* You know that his clinic record card bears the notation *heart murmur.*
    Under these circumstances, it would be BEST for you to tell him

    A. he has a heart murmur, since he obviously knows this and his card gives you the information
    B. he does not have a heart condition, since the doctor would have informed the patient if he wanted him to know about it

C. not to worry about it since lots of people have a heart condition
D. to ask the physician whom he has been seeing in the clinic about this

15. If a 3-year-old child refuses to stay on a scale long enough to be weighed, the BEST of the following actions for you to take is to

    A. obtain the child's weight by first weighing the mother holding the child in her arms, and then weighing the mother alone
    B. insist that the child be weighed so that the other children in the clinic will cooperate when being weighed
    C. ask one of the special officers to assist her in weighing the child
    D. note on the record that the child refused to be weighed and let the physician determine if it is necessary to weigh the child

16. You have been asked to hand the sterile instruments to the physician while he is changing a dressing. Suppose that halfway through the procedure, the doctor drops the forceps he is using.
    Of the following actions, the one that you should take at this time is to

    A. pick up the forceps with your hand and ask the doctor if he will need it any more
    B. pick up the forceps with your hand and place it with other contaminated instruments
    C. move the forceps out of the way with your foot
    D. use sterile forceps from the cabinet to pick up the forceps from the floor

17. You have been asked to prepare a list of supplies to be reordered for your clinic.
    In order for you to determine how much of any item to reorder, it would be MOST important to know

    A. the average amount of the item used in a given period of time
    B. what the item is used for in the clinic
    C. how much storage space is available for these supplies
    D. the cost of each item

18. Assume that when you open a cabinet in which disinfectants are kept, you find that one of the bottles has no label. However, there is a label on the shelf near the bottle.
    Of the following, the BEST action for you to take is to

    A. paste the label on the bottle since it obviously is the label for that bottle
    B. paste the label on the bottle only if the label has the word *disinfectant* clearly marked on it
    C. place the bottle back in the cabinet and ask the nurse in charge what to do
    D. pour the contents of the bottle into the sink, rinse the bottle, and place it in the proper receptacle

19. After washing and rinsing rubber hot water bottles, hang then upside down with their mouths open. When they are thoroughly dry, inflate them, place the stoppers into the mouths of the bottles, and leave them hanging. If they are to be stored, leave them inflated and place gauze or crushed paper between them.
    On the basis of this paragraph, the one of the following statements that is MOST accurate is that, when storing hot water bottles,

A. they should be stuffed with paper
B. a free flow of air must circulate around them
C. care must be taken to prevent their sides from sticking together
D. they should be placed upside down with their mouths open

20. In filing, a cross index should be used for a record which 20.____

    A. may be filed in either of two places
    B. has been temporarily removed from the file
    C. concerns a patient who is no longer coming to the clinic
    D. will be used to remind patients of appointments

21. Assume that the cards of patients are kept in alphabetical order. You are given an alphabetical list of persons who have received injections for *Asian flu* at the clinic, and are asked to see if there is a card in the file for each person on the list.
    It would be BEST for you to 21.____

    A. determine if the number of cards and the number of names on the list are the same
    B. place a check mark next to each name on the list for which there is a corresponding card
    C. place a check mark on each card for which there is a corresponding name on the list
    D. prepare a second list of all cards in the file and place a check mark next to each name for which there is a corresponding name on the first list

22. Assume that there are several clinics within a health center. Patients' cards are filed according to the clinic which they attend, and within each clinic are filed alphabetically. Every Friday you are responsible for filing the cards of all patients who were in the health center during that week. The cards are in mixed order.
    Of the following, the FIRST step to take is to 22.____

    A. arrange the patients' cards in alphabetical order
    B. separate the cards of those patients who attended more than one clinic from all the others
    C. arrange the patients' cards according to the clinic attended
    D. arrange the patients' cards according to the date the patient attended the clinic

23. Suppose that, in Clinic A, a medical history card is prepared for each new patient. In this clinic, a blood test is made for each patient as a routine procedure. You have been instructed to make out either a blue card for a negative report, or a white card for a positive report, when the laboratory reports of the blood tests are received.
    In order to make sure that all reports on the blood tests have been received, you should compare the number of reports received with the number of _____ cards. 23.____

    A. medical history   B. blue
    C. white   D. blue and white

24. Assume that you are in charge of ordering supplies needed for the clinic. When reordering items, it is BEST to 24.____

A. count supplies at the beginning of each month and reorder an item as soon as there is no more of it in stock
B. determine beforehand the amount of each item which it is necessary to have on hand and reorder the item when the supply falls to this level
C. reorder each item in sufficient quantity to last half a year so that there will be no danger of running out of supplies
D. reorder all items at the beginning of each month so that no item needed will be forgotten

25. It is usually recommended that, when new supplies of any item are received, they be placed beneath or behind supplies of the item already in stock.
Of the following, the BEST reason for this is that this procedure

   A. requires less frequent handling of supplies
   B. makes it easier to tell how much of each item you have on hand
   C. allows you to use the storage space most effectively
   D. makes it more likely that the older supplies will be used first

26. The abbreviation *EEG* refers to a(n)

   A. examination of the eyes and ears
   B. inflammatory disease of the urinogenital tract
   C. disease of the esophageal structure
   D. examination of the brain

27. The complete destruction of all forms of living microorganisms is called

   A. decontamination   B. fumigation
   C. sterilization   D. germination

28. A rectal thermometer differs from other fever thermometers in that it has a

   A. longer stem   B. thinner stem
   C. stubby bulb at one end D. slender bulb at one end

29. The one of the following pieces of equipment which is usually used together with a sphygmometer is a

   A. stethoscope   B. watch
   C. fever thermometer   D. hypodermic syringe

30. A curette is a

   A. healing drug   B. curved scalpel
   C. long hypodermic needle D. scraping instrument

31. The otoscope is used to examine the patient's

   A. eyes   B. ears   C. mouth   D. lungs

32. A catheter is used

   A. to close wounds
   B. for withdrawing fluid from a body cavity
   C. to remove cataracts
   D. as a cathartic

33. Of the following pieces of equipment, the one that is required for making a scratch test is a   33.____

    A. needle   B. scalpel
    C. capillary tube   D. tourniquet

34. A hemostat is an instrument which is used to   34.____

    A. hold a sterile needle
    B. clamp off a blood vessel
    C. regulate the temperature of a sterilizer
    D. measure oxygen intake

35. Of the following medical supplies, the one that MUST be stored in a tightly sealed bottle is   35.____

    A. sodium fluoride
    B. alum
    C. oil of cloves
    D. aromatic spirits of ammonia

36. A person who has been exposed to an infectious disease is called   36.____

    A. a contact   B. an incubator
    C. diseased   D. infected

37. A myocardial infarct would occur in the   37.____

    A. heart   B. kidneys   C. lungs   D. spleen

38. The abbreviations *WBC* and *RBC* refer to the results of tests of the   38.____

    A. basal metabolism   B. blood
    C. blood pressure   D. bony structure

39. When a person's blood pressure is noted as 120/80, it means that his _____ blood pressure is _____.   39.____

    A. pulse; 120   B. pulse; 80
    C. systolic; 120   D. systolic; 80

40. The anatomical structure that contains the tonsils and adenoids is the   40.____

    A. pharynx   B. larynx   C. trachea   D. sinuses

41. An abscess can BEST be described as a   41.____

    A. loss of sensation
    B. painful tooth
    C. ruptured membrane
    D. localized formation of pus

42. Nephritis is a disease affecting the   42.____

    A. gall bladder   B. larynx
    C. kidney   D. large intestine

43. Hemoglobin is contained in the

    A. white blood cells
    B. lymph fluids
    C. platelets
    D. red blood cells

44. Bile is a body fluid that is MOST directly concerned with

    A. digestion
    B. excretion
    C. reproduction
    D. metabolism

45. Of the following bones, the one which is located below the waist is the

    A. sternum
    B. clavicle
    C. tibia
    D. humerus

46. The one of the following which is NOT part of the digestive canal is the

    A. esophagus
    B. larynx
    C. duodenum
    D. colon

47. The thyroid and the pituitary are part of the _____ system.

    A. digestive
    B. endocrine
    C. respiratory
    D. excretory

48. The one of the following which would be included in a *GU* examination is the

    A. rectum
    B. trachea
    C. kidneys
    D. pancreas

49. Of the following, the one which would be included in the x-ray examination known as a *GI series* is the

    A. colon
    B. skull
    C. lungs
    D. uterus

50. A person who, while not ill himself, may transmit a disease to another person is known as a(n)

    A. breeder
    B. incubator
    C. carrier
    D. inhibitor

KEY (CORRECT ANSWERS)

1. D	11. B	21. B	31. B	41. D
2. C	12. A	22. C	32. B	42. C
3. A	13. B	23. A	33. A	43. D
4. A	14. D	24. B	34. B	44. A
5. D	15. A	25. D	35. D	45. C
6. C	16. C	26. D	36. A	46. B
7. B	17. A	27. C	37. A	47. B
8. A	18. D	28. C	38. B	48. C
9. C	19. C	29. A	39. C	49. A
10. C	20. A	30. D	40. A	50. C

TEST 2

DIRECTIONS: Each question or incomplete statement is followed by several suggested answers or completions. Select the one that BEST answers the question or completes the statement. *PRINT THE LETTER OF THE CORRECT ANSWER IN THE SPACE AT THE RIGHT.*

1. Thorough washing of the hands for two minutes with soap and warm water will leave the hands 1.____
    - A. sterile
    - B. aseptic
    - C. decontaminated
    - D. partially disinfected

2. The one of the following which is BEST for preparing the skin for an injection is 2.____
    - A. green soap and water
    - B. alcohol
    - C. phenol
    - D. formalin

3. A fever thermometer should be cleansed after use by washing it with 3.____
    - A. soap and cool water
    - B. warm water only
    - C. soap and hot water
    - D. running cold tap water

4. The FIRST step in cleaning an instrument which has fresh blood on it is to 4.____
    - A. wash it in hot soapy water
    - B. wash it under cool running water
    - C. soak it in a boric acid bath
    - D. soak it in 70% alcohol

5. If a contaminated nasal speculum cannot be sterilized immediately after use, then the BEST procedure to follow until sterilization is possible is to place it 5.____
    - A. under a piece of dry gauze
    - B. in warm water
    - C. in alcohol
    - D. in a green soap solution

6. A hypodermic needle should always be checked to see if it has a good sharp point 6.____
    - A. when it is being washed
    - B. when it is removed from the sterilizer
    - C. just before it is sterilized
    - D. immediately before an injection

7. Of the following, the LOWEST temperature at which cotton goods will be sterilized if placed in an autoclave for 30 minutes is _____ °F. 7.____
    - A. 130
    - B. 170
    - C. 200
    - D. 250

8. Of the following procedures, the one which is BEST for sterilizing an ear speculum which is contaminated with wax is to 8.____

A. scrub in with cold soapy water, rinse in ether, and place in boiling water for 20 minutes
B. soak it in warm water, scrub in cold soapy water, rinse with water, and autoclave at 275°F for 10 minutes
C. wash it in alcohol, scrub in hot soapy water, rinse with water, and place in boiling water for 20 minutes
D. wash it in 1% Lysol solution, rinse, and autoclave at 275°F for 15 minutes

9. Assume that clean water accidentally spilled on the outside of a package of cloth-wrapped hypodermic syringes which has been sterilized.
Of the following, the BEST action to take is to

    A. leave the package to dry in a sunny, clean place
    B. sterilize the package again
    C. remove the wet cloth and wrap the package in a dry sterile cloth
    D. wipe off the package with a clean dry towel and later ask the nurse in charge what to do

10. Hypodermic needles should be sterilized by placing them in

    A. boiling water for 5 minutes
    B. an autoclave at 15 lbs. pressure for 15 minutes
    C. oil heated to 220°F for 10 minutes
    D. a 1:40 Lysol solution for 10 minutes

11. A cutting instrument should be sterilized by placing it in

    A. a chemical germicide
    B. an autoclave at 15 lbs. pressure for 20 minutes
    C. boiling water for 20 minutes
    D. a hot air oven at 320°F for 1 hour

12. A fever thermometer used by a patient who has tuberculosis should be washed and then placed in _____ minute(s).

    A. boiling water for 10
    B. a hot air oven for 20
    C. a 1:1000 solution of bichloride of mercury for one
    D. an autoclave at 15 lbs. pressure for 15

13. The MOST reliable method of sterilizing a glass syringe is to place it in _____ minutes.

    A. Zephiran chloride 1:1000 solution for 40
    B. oil heated to 250°F for 12
    C. boiling water for 20
    D. an autoclave at 15 lbs. pressure for 20

14. The insides of sterilizers should be cleaned daily with a mild abrasive PRIMARILY to

    A. remove scale
    B. prevent the growth of bacteria
    C. remove blood and other organic matter
    D. prevent acids from damaging the sterilizer

15. Of the following, the BEST reason for giving a patient a jar in which to bring a urine specimen on his next visit to the clinic is that the

    A. patient may not have a jar at home
    B. patient may bring the specimen in a jar which is too large
    C. patient may bring the specimen in a jar which has not been cleaned properly
    D. jar may be misplaced if it is not a jar in which urine specimens are usually collected

15.____

16. Simply providing nutritional information and recommended low-cost diets to clinic patients has not resulted in improved diets for their children.
    The MOST plausible conclusion to draw from this statement is that

    A. nutrition is only one factor in improving health
    B. nutrition is of greater value in improving the health of adults than in improving the health of children
    C. the health problems of clinic patients are not caused by nutritional defects
    D. clinic patients are not using the nutritional information given them

16.____

17. Many people who appear to be robust are highly susceptible to disease, and are outlived by many seemingly frail people.
    Of the following, the MOST plausible conclusion which may be drawn from this statement is that

    A. physical appearance is not a reliable indicator of health
    B. frail people take better care of themselves than do robust people
    C. disease tends to strike robust people more frequently than frail people
    D. robust people tend to overexert themselves more often than frail people do

17.____

18. The skill of interviewers, the wording of questions, and the willingness of patients to respond freely to questions all affect the results of a survey. Reports of surveys of patient attitudes toward the health work of the clinic are, therefore, valueless unless we also know how the surveys were conducted. A recent report that 85% of clinic patients were satisfied with clinic service must be treated with caution; it may be that another survey would have revealed just the opposite!
    On the basis of this paragraph, it is MOST accurate to conclude that

    A. survey reports have little value in determining patient attitudes
    B. contrary to a recent report, 85% of clinic patients are dissatisfied with clinic service
    C. published results of surveys may be misleading unless accompanied by knowledge of the methods used
    D. listening to the unsolicited comments of clinic patients is of greater value than questioning them directly concerning their attitudes

18.____

Questions 19-25.

DIRECTIONS: Questions 19 through 25 are to be answered on the basis of the following table

STATISTICAL REPORT OF CLINICS IN XYZ HEALTH CENTER March				
	APPOINTMENTS		PROCEDURES	
Clinic	No. of Appointments Scheduled	No. of Broken Appointments	No. of Diagnostic Procedures	No. of Surgical Procedures
A	1400	260	1910	140
B	730	160	2000	500
C	1250	250	950	130
D	540	90	400	220
E	890	140	1500	280

19. On the basis of the preceding table, the total number of appointments kept for all clinics in the health center in March is

    A. 900 B. 3910 C. 4810 D. 5710

20. The percentage of appointments kept in Clinic C during March is

    A. 5% B. 20% C. 75% D. 80%

21. If Clinic A was open for 20 days during March, the average number of appointments scheduled each day at Clinic A is

    A. 57 B. 70 C. 140 D. 280

22. In comparison to the clinic which performed the fewest diagnostic procedures, the clinic which performed the MOST diagnostic procedures did _____ as many.

    A. twice
    C. four times
    B. three times
    D. five times

23. The average number of diagnostic procedures performed for all clinics during March is

    A. 254 B. 676 C. 1352 D. 6760

24. The percentage of all procedures done at Clinic B during March which were surgical procedures is

    A. 2% B. 2.5% C. 20% D. 25%

25. Clinic E used 10 boxes of gauze for its surgical procedures during March. If Clinic A used gauze at the same rate for its surgical procedures, the number of boxes of gauze Clinic A used during March is

    A. 3 B. 5 C. 10 D. 14

Questions 26-34.

DIRECTIONS: Each of Questions 26 through 34 consists of four words. Three of these words belong together. One word does NOT belong with the other three. For each group of words, you are to select the one word which does NOT belong with the other three words.

26. A. conclude B. terminate C. initiate D. end 26.____
27. A. deficient B. inadequate 27.____
    C. excessive D. insufficient
28. A. rare B. unique C. unusual D. frequent 28.____
29. A. unquestionable B. uncertain 29.____
    C. doubtful D. indefinite
30. A. stretch B. contract C. extend D. expand 30.____
31. A. accelerate B. quicken 31.____
    C. accept D. hasten
32. A. sever B. rupture C. rectify D. tear 32.____
33. A. innocuous B. injurious C. dangerous D. harmful 33.____
34. A. adulterate B. contaminate 34.____
    C. taint D. disinfect

Questions 35-40.

DIRECTIONS: Questions 35 through 40 are to be answered on the basis of the usual rules for alphabetical filing. For each question, indicate in the space at the right the letter preceding the name which should be filed THIRD in alphabetical order.

35. A. Russell Cohen B. Henry Cohn 35.____
    C. Wesley Chambers D. Arthur Connors
36. A. Wanda Jenkins B. Pauline Jennings 36.____
    C. Leslie Jantzenberg D. Rudy Jensen
37. A. Arnold Wilson B. Carlton Willson 37.____
    C. Duncan Williamson D. Ezra Wilston
38. A. Joseph M. Buchman B. Gustave Bozzerman 38.____
    C. Constantino Brunelli D. Armando Buccino
39. A. Barbara Waverly B. Corinne Warterdam 39.____
    C. Dennis Waterman D. Harold Wartman
40. A. Jose Mejia B. Bernard Mendelsohn 40.____
    C. Antonio Mejias D. Richard Mazzitelli

Questions 41-50.

DIRECTIONS: Questions 41 through 50 are to be answered on the basis of the usual rules of filing. Column I lists, next to the numbers 91 to 100, the names of 10 clinic patients. Column II lists, next to the letters A to D, the headings of file drawers into which you are to place the records of these patients. For each question, indicate in the space at the right the letter preceding the heading of the file drawer in which the record should be filed.

COLUMN I

41. Frank Shea
42. Rose Seaborn
43. Samuel Smollin
44. Thomas Shur
45. Ben Schaefer
46. Shirley Strauss
47. Harry Spiro
48. Dora Skelly
49. Sylvia Smith
50. Arnold Selz

COLUMN II

A. Sab - Sej
B. Sek - Sio
C. Sip - Soo
D. Sop - Syz

41.___
42.___
43.___
44.___
45.___
46.___
47.___
48.___
49.___
50.___

KEY (CORRECT ANSWERS)

1.	D	11.	A	21.	B	31.	C	41.	B
2.	B	12.	C	22.	D	32.	C	42.	A
3.	A	13.	D	23.	C	33.	A	43.	C
4.	B	14.	A	24.	C	34.	D	44.	B
5.	D	15.	C	25.	B	35.	B	45.	A
6.	C	16.	D	26.	C	36.	B	46.	D
7.	D	17.	A	27.	C	37.	A	47.	D
8.	C	18.	C	28.	D	38.	D	48.	C
9.	B	19.	B	29.	A	39.	C	49.	C
10.	B	20.	D	30.	B	40.	C	50.	B

EXAMINATION SECTION
TEST 1

DIRECTIONS: Each question or incomplete statement is followed by several suggested answers or completions. Select the one that BEST answers the question or completes the statement. *PRINT THE LETTER OF THE CORRECT ANSWER IN THE SPACE AT THE RIGHT.*

1. Of the following, the one which is NOT considered to be a duty of the assistant is to   1.____

    A. interview the patients
    B. administer local anaesthesia to a patient
    C. take the temperature of patients
    D. aid the patient in preparing for a medical examination

2. Assume that a patient appears at your clinic at 11:00 on a busy day while you are on duty   2.____
in the reception room. He says that he missed his 9:00 appointment and that he must return to work within an hour.
The one of the following which is the MOST acceptable course of action for you to take FIRST is to

    A. ask the others who are waiting if they will allow this patient to precede them
    B. immediately schedule another appointment for the patient for the same day in the following week
    C. take the patient to the examining room to see the doctor immediately
    D. explain to the patient that others are waiting and ask him to wait his turn

3. As an assistant, you will be required to follow certain instructions of the doctor or nurse in   3.____
the administration of the clinic. Suppose that you have been given some instructions by the doctor which you do not completely understand.
The one of the following which is the MOST advisable course of conduct for you to follow is to

    A. carry out the instructions to the best of your ability
    B. ask another employee in the clinic to interpret the order to you
    C. ask the doctor to repeat the instructions or to clarify them
    D. disregard the instructions and wait until the doctor speaks to you again

4. As the assistant assigned to a district health center, you are required to interview new   4.____
patients briefly to determine which clinics they are to go to. There are a number of patients waiting to talk to you. The person whom you are interviewing is Italian and speaks English so poorly that it is almost impossible for you to understand her. She is also very upset and excited. You know that one of the clerks in the eye clinic speaks Italian.
For you to call that clerk and ask him to act as interpreter is

    A. *inadvisable;* the information you must get is confidential and should not be known to the clerk
    B. *advisable* ; the person you are interviewing will be more comfortable in her own language and the interview will, therefore, be completed more quickly
    C. *inadvisable;* the clerk you wish to call may not want to act as interpreter
    D. *advisable;* you will not be responsible for any misunderstanding in this situation if someone else did the interviewing

15

5. You are assigned to a chest clinic. One Saturday morning, you are alone in the clinic. The doctor has telephoned that he will be delayed and the nurse has not yet reported. One of the regular clinic patients begins coughing while she is talking to you and has a severe hemorrhage.
The BEST procedure for you to follow in this situation is to

   A. give the patient a stimulant and apply a cold compress to the back of the neck
   B. look in the other clinics to see if there is anyone else on duty
   C. do nothing until the doctor comes in
   D. call the police for an ambulance

6. Suppose that you are assigned to interviewing incoming patients for certain routine information in a busy dental clinic. You learn that some patients go to the eye clinic after you have interviewed them where another assistant interviews them for the same information. The two sets of information are to be kept in permanent card files, in two separate clinic offices.
Of the following suggestions which you might make to your supervisor, the one which would prove to be MOST helpful in simplifying this procedure would be for you to

   A. continue to record the information separately so that you can check your records with those of the other assistant for possible errors
   B. send the patient to the other clinic first since they may need more information than you do
   C. fill out two record cards and forward one card to the other clinic
   D. send your record card to the other clinic with the patient after he has been examined by the doctor

7. Suppose that a visitor calls at your clinic and requests information concerning the medical history of a patient. Of the following, the MOST acceptable action for you to take is to

   A. ask him why he wants the information so that you may determine if there is sufficient reason for you to give him the information
   B. give him the information readily as this will foster favorable public relations
   C. refer him to the doctor who examined the patient as he is in a better position to know the patient's medical history
   D. explain that you cannot give out such information as it is strictly confidential and suggest that he write to the department for the information

8. To equip a corner of the outer office of a health center with toys is

   A. *advisable;* the children will be occupied while waiting and, therefore, will be more manageable during the doctor's examination and treatment
   B. *inadvisable;* the child may become too absorbed in play to submit to examination
   C. *advisable;* the children will be so absorbed in play that they will not be aware of whatever discomfort is caused by treatment
   D. *inadvisable;* playing may overstimulate the child and thus cause inaccurate results in the examination

9. While working in a clinic, you discover some obvious inconsistencies in the filing system as a whole. You also have in mind a corrective measure which you would like to see put into practice.
   The one of the following which is the MOST acceptable procedure for you to follow is to

   A. try out your new system for a few days to determine its success before discussing it with your supervisor
   B. explain the probable advantages of your proposed plan to your supervisor and secure his approval before making any changes
   C. continue working under the old procedure until the inconsistencies become apparent to the rest of the staff
   D. collect sufficient evidence to prove the obvious inconsistencies in the present filing system in order to convince your supervisor that the system is unsatisfactory

10. Assume that you are in charge of the patients' files in the health center to which you are assigned. The record cards of the individual patients are filed alphabetically according to the name of the patient. You want to make it easier to pick out the cards of those patients who are under treatment for any one of five indicated diseases. Of the following, the procedure which would be MOST helpful for this purpose would be to

    A. insert the card of each patient having one of the five diseases into a special folder
    B. use a different size card for each of the five diseases
    C. use a different color card for each of the five diseases
    D. underline the name of the disease on each card in the file

11. Assume that you are assigned to the chest clinic where you are responsible for the patients' x-ray records. The doctor in charge tells you that in an old group of about 250 disarranged pictures, he thinks there may be several instances in which more than one record exists for the same patient. He asks you to pick out any such records and give them to him.
    Of the following, the BEST procedure for you to follow FIRST is to

    A. look at each record in turn, number it, and make a list of the numbers and corresponding names
    B. go through the records quickly and pick out those names which you remember
    C. arrange the records in alphabetical order according to the names of the patients
    D. list the names of all the patients whose records appear in the group

12. As an assistant, one of your principal duties is the proper maintenance of the supply cabinet of the clinic to which you are assigned. Upon inspecting the cabinet, you find several large containers with identical labels. However, these contain pills of different color and shapes. Of the following, the MOST acceptable course of conduct for you to follow is to

    A. attempt to sort the pills and relabel them on the basis of your own knowledge
    B. throw all of the pills away to make certain they will not be misused
    C. inform the doctor that you have relabeled the containers after sorting the pills
    D. inform the doctor of the situation so that he may decide what is to be done

13. Assume that a patient arrives at the clinic and demands an immediate appointment at a time when the doctor is busy.
Of the following, the action which is MOST acceptable for you to take is to

    A. give the patient a sedative to quiet his nerves and guide him to an unoccupied examination room to rest
    B. explain to the patient that the doctor is busy and ask him to be seated in the waiting room
    C. ask the doctor to examine the patient immediately
    D. talk to the patient until the doctor is ready

14. One of your duties in the clinic is the weighing and measurement of adult patients.
Of the following, the procedure which is NOT necessary to secure accurate weighing of patients is

    A. daily testing and adjustment of the scale for accurate balance
    B. instructing the patient to stand firmly in the center of the scale
    C. noting what type of clothing the patient is wearing
    D. placing a clean paper towel on the scale before each patient is weighed

15. Suppose that a patient in the clinic is in immediate need of first aid for shock.
The MOST important thing to do first when both the doctor and nurse are absent is to

    A. make the patient as comfortable as possible and administer a sedative
    B. keep the patient on his feet and moving about in order to activate blood circulation throughout the body
    C. keep the patient as warm as possible
    D. try to locate the doctor before attempting any independent action

16. A patient reports for her scheduled appointment in the pre-natal clinic and tells you, while she is waiting to be examined, that she has a very severe pain in her back. Of the following, the MOST acceptable action for you to take is to

    A. express sympathy and tell her that you yourself once had a severe backache for which it was difficult to get any relief
    B. tell her politely not to take up your time with her ailments as you have other things to do
    C. recommend a liniment which you have used and found to be very helpful in such cases
    D. suggest that she speak to the doctor about it when he examines her

17. A *ticketer system* in a health center may be used as a

    A. follow-up procedure for the recall of patients
    B. method of charting blood pressure recordings at each visit
    C. standard procedure for recording information to be included in memoranda to the doctors
    D. series of tests of nervous reactions

18. When papers are filed according to the date of their receipt, they are said to be filed

    A. numerically   B. geographically
    C. chronologically   D. alphabetically

19. The one of the following which is the MOST important requirement of a good filing system is that   19._____

   A. the expense of installation and operation be low
   B. papers be found easily when needed
   C. the system be capable of any amount of expansion which may be necessary in the future
   D. the filing system have a cross-reference index

Questions 20-24.

DIRECTIONS: Questions 20 through 24 consist of a group of names which are to be arranged in alphabetical order for filing.

20. Of the following, the name which should be filed FIRST is   20._____

   A. Joseph J. Meadeen   B. Gerard L. Meader
   C. John F. Madcar   D. Philip F. Malder

21. Of the following, the name which should be filed LAST is   21._____

   A. Stephen Fischer   B. Benjamin Fitchmann
   C. Thomas Fishman   D. Augustus S. Fisher

22. The name which should be filed SECOND is   22._____

   A. Yeatman, Frances   B. Yeaton, C.S.
   C. Yeatman, R.M.   D. Yeats, John

23. The name which should be filed THIRD is   23._____

   A. Hauser, Ann   B. Hauptmann, Jane
   C. Hauster, Mary   D. Hauprich, Julia

24. The name which should be filed SECOND is   24._____

   A. Flora McDougall   B. Fred E. MacDowell
   C. Juanita Mendez   D. James A. Madden

25. The *initial* contact is of great importance in setting a pattern for future relations.   25._____
    The word *initial,* as used in this sentence, means MOST NEARLY

   A. first   B. written   C. direct   D. hidden

26. The doctor prescribed a diet which was *adequate* for the patient's needs.   26._____
    The word *adequate,* as used in this sentence, means MOST NEARLY

   A. insufficient   B. unusual
   C. required   D. enough

27. The child was reported to be suffering from a vitamin *deficiency.*   27._____
    The word *deficiency,* as used in this sentence, means MOST NEARLY

   A. surplus   B. infection   C. shortage   D. injury

28. In obtaining medical case data, a medical record librarian should discourage the patient from giving *irrelevant* information.
    The word *irrelevant*, as used in this sentence means MOST NEARLY

    A. too detailed
    B. pertaining to relatives
    C. insufficient
    D. inappropriate

29. The doctor requested that a *tentative* appointment be made for the patient.
    The word *tentative*, as used in this sentence, means MOST NEARLY

    A. definite
    B. subject to change
    C. later
    D. of short duration

30. The black plague resulted in an usually high *mortality rate* in the population of Europe.
    The term *mortality rate*, as used in this sentence, means MOST NEARLY

    A. future immunity of the people
    B. death rate
    C. general weakening of the health of the people
    D. sickness rate

31. The public health assistant was asked to file a number of *identical* reports on the case.
    The word *identical*, as used in this sentence, means MOST NEARLY

    A. accurate   B. detailed   C. same   D. different

32. The nurse assisted in the *biopsy* of the patient.
    The word *biopsy*, as used in this sentence, means MOST NEARLY

    A. autopsy
    B. excision and diagnostic study of tissue
    C. biography and health history
    D. administering of anesthesia

33. The assistant noted that the swelling on the patient's face had *subsided*.
    The word *subsided*, as used in this sentence, means MOST NEARLY

    A. become aggravated
    B. increased
    C. vanished
    D. abated

34. The patient was given food *intravenously*.
    The word *intravenously*, as used in this sentence, means MOST NEARLY

    A. orally
    B. against his will
    C. through the veins
    D. without condiment

Questions 35-40.

DIRECTIONS: Questions 35 through 40 are to be answered on the basis of the chart below.

SEMI-ANNUAL REPORT OF EXPENDITURES FOR SUPPLIES AND EQUIPMENT
Health Center X - January to June

MONTH	CLINIC					
	BABY	CHEST	DENTAL	PRE-NATAL	X-RAY	TOTAL
January	$456.32	$204.28	$723.22	$436.29	$153.25	$1,973.36
February	425.59	225.27	743.33	452.51	174.42	2,021.12
March	631.93	226.35	716.29	429.33	173.37	2,177.27
April	587.27	321.42	729.37	397.27	185.28	2,220.61
May	535.22	275.52	750.54	335.23	184.97	2,081.48
June	539.20	226.80	755.67	394.25	181.08	2,097.00
Total	$3,175.53	$1,479.64	$4,418.42	$2,444.88	$1,052.37	$12,570.84

35. On the basis of the above chart, the TOTAL expenses of the dental clinic exceed the total expenses of the baby clinic for the six-month period by   35.____

   A. $1,242.89   B. $1,243.79   C. $1,342.79   D. $1,343.89

36. The total expenses for the month of January for Health Center X EXCEED the total expenses of the chest clinic for the six-month period by   36.____

   A. $473.82   B. $483.72   C. $484.72   D. $493.72

37. The expenditures for the entire Health Center were HIGHEST during the month of   37.____

   A. February   B. March   C. April   D. June

38. If the total number of patients treated at the Health Center during February was 632, the APPROXIMATE cost per patient for the month of February is   38.____

   A. $3.20   B. $12.50   C. $21.00   D. $31.90

39. The TOTAL expenditure for the dental clinic for the six-month period is   39.____

   A. *more* than double the total expenses of the Health Center for March
   B. *less* than one-fourth the total expenses of the Health Center for the six-month period
   C. *more* than double the total expenses of the Health Center for April
   D. *less* than the combined totals for the six-month period of expenses for the baby and x-ray clinics

40. The TOTAL expenditure for the first three months for the baby clinic is   40.____

   A. *greater* than the total expenses for the baby clinic for the last three months
   B. *less* than the total expenses for the chest clinic for the entire six-month period
   C. *less* than the total expenses for the baby clinic for the last three months
   D. *greater* than the total expenses for the pre-natal clinic for the entire six-month period

KEY (CORRECT ANSWERS)

1. B	11. C	21. B	31. C
2. A	12. D	22. C	32. B
3. C	13. B	23. A	33. D
4. B	14. D	24. D	34. C
5. D	15. C	25. A	35. A
6. C	16. D	26. D	36. D
7. D	17. A	27. C	37. C
8. A	18. C	28. D	38. A
9. B	19. B	29. B	39. A
10. C	20. C	30. B	40. C

TEST 2

DIRECTIONS: Each question or incomplete statement is followed by several suggested answers or completions. Select the one that BEST answers the question or completes the statement. *PRINT THE LETTER OF THE CORRECT ANSWER IN THE SPACE AT THE RIGHT.*

1. For an employee to address callers at the clinic by name is 1.____

    A. *advisable;* this is a courtesy that everyone appreciates
    B. *inadvisable;* it would be very embarrassing if she greeted a patient by the wrong name
    C. *advisable;* this assures the patient that the assistant is concentrating on her work
    D. *inadvisable;* patients will tend to take advantage of this display of familiarity

2. One of your duties is to get certain preliminary information from a new patient before giving him or her an appointment with the doctor for a later day. The data are to be entered on a permanent record card. Assume that you are interviewing a woman who speaks very broken English and asks if she can talk to you in Spanish. You speak some Spanish and are able to get most of the information from her, but are unable to understand a few of her answers. 2.____
The one of the following which is the BEST action for you to take is to

    A. tell the woman you can't understand her and ask her to come back with an interpreter
    B. fill in on the card all the necessary data as best you can
    C. fill in the information you are certain to have understood correctly, and, at the time of the next appointment, point out to the doctor the omissions
    D. write out for the woman the questions you have not answered on the card and ask her to bring back the answers in writing, in English, the next time she comes

3. Assume that the doctor who is to take charge of the morning session of your clinic has been unavoidably detained and arrives an hour late, at 10 A.M. 3.____
The one of the following which is the BEST action for you to take is to

    A. ask the patients who have arrived for the appointment between 9 and 10:00 to come back at another time
    B. ask all patients if they can wait; if not, give them appointments for another time
    C. say nothing to any of the patients
    D. ask the patients who had appointments for the last hour of the session to come back at another time

4. Assume that you are put in charge of a medicine supply cabinet and you note two identical bottles, one containing a harmless liquid, the other a poisonous substance. You should 4.____

    A. make certain that both bottles are clearly labeled at all times
    B. make certain that the bottle containing the poisonous substance is clearly labeled at all times
    C. pour the liquids over into different shaped bottles
    D. keep the bottles on two different shelves

23

5. Assume that a patient with a painful shoulder comes in during the doctor's absence and asks you to give him a treatment such as the doctor had prescribed for him some months earlier.
   You should

   A. comply with the request since the difficulty is obviously a relapse
   B. give the patient a sedative and suggest that he call for a future appointment if the pain does not subside
   C. ask him to return later when the doctor will be in
   D. explain that, since you are not a registered nurse, you are not qualified to give treatment

6. A patient telephones the clinic before the doctor arrives and says that the medicine the doctor prescribed for her makes her nauseous. She wants to know whether she should continue taking it.
   The one of the following steps which you should take FIRST is to

   A. advise her to stop taking the medication if it is not effective
   B. suggest that she continue taking the medicine for another week to see if the nausea stops
   C. say that you will inform the doctor and call her back
   D. recommend that she check the accuracy of the prescription with the pharmacist

7. Assume that one of the medicines in your supply cabinet is one which deteriorates within a certain period of time, and becomes ineffective after that time. According to instructions, you reorder the medicine periodically, so that when the old supply becomes ineffective a fresh supply is on hand. You find, however, that only a small quantity from each bottle is being used, and the major portion has to be thrown away.
   The one of the following which is the BEST procedure for you to follow is to

   A. continue to order as before, since you cannot prevent the medicine from spoiling
   B. wait with the fresh order until the old supply has been used up
   C. order periodically as before, but in smaller quantities
   D. order periodically, but at greater intervals, so that more of the medicine will be used up

8. Assume that you are charged with the weekly weighing of a certain group of children attending your clinic. Your doctor instructs you to fill out a certain card form for any child whose weight differs by 5% or more from the previous week's reading. One morning, you weigh five of these children. Child A weighs 63 lbs., B, 54 lbs., C, 47 1/2 lbs., D, 57 lbs., and E, 61 lbs. The previous week's readings were: A, 65 lbs.; B, 51 lbs.; C, 50 lbs.; D, 59 1/2 lbs.; E, 56 1/2 lbs.
   The children for whom you will make out cards will be

   A. A, B, and C   B. B and E
   C. A, C, D, and E   D. B, C, and E

9. A mother comes to the health center with an infant who appears to be ill. As she comes in, she tells you she believes the child may have caught the measles from a neighbor's child who is just recovering from the disease. The BEST of the following actions for you to take is to

   A. tell the mother to take a seat and wait her turn to see the doctor

B. ask the mother if she wants to take a chance on a cancelled appointment, as the doctor's schedule is filled for the day
C. scold the mother for coming in without an appointment and arrange for an appointment on the next clinic day
D. take the mother and child into a vacant examination room and inform the doctor at once

10. Assume that you notice that one of the drugs in your supply cabinet has changed color. It is not on the list of drugs which deteriorate and which must be reordered periodically. The one of the following which is the BEST action for you to take is to

    A. order a new supply of the drug immediately
    B. report the matter to the doctor immediately
    C. ignore the change in the drug, as it is not caused by deterioration
    D. point out the change to the doctor the next time he asks for the drug

11. To use screw caps on medicine bottles in preference to glass stoppers is

    A. *wise*; screw caps are more attractive
    B. *unwise*; glass stoppers are less expensive
    C. *wise*; screw caps afford more protection to the lip of the bottle
    D. *unwise*; glass stoppers are often interchangeable for several bottles

12. The one of the following which is the LEAST important precaution to take in connection with the pouring of a dose of medicine from a bottle into a glass is to

    A. wear sterile rubber gloves while pouring
    B. hold the label on the bottle uppermost while pouring
    C. clean the rim of the bottle after pouring
    D. make certain the medicine isn't left around for any time in an unmarked glass

13. To cover a typed label on a medicine bottle with shellac is

    A. *inadvisable*; the shellac may have a chemical reaction on the drug
    B. *advisable*; the label will become waterproof and the printing on it remain legible
    C. *inadvisable*; the shellac will cause the printing on the label to become illegible
    D. *advisable*; the shellac will prevent the bottle from breaking in case it is dropped

14. The one of the following which is the MOST valid reason for a patient's needing a prescription in order to obtain a certain drug is that the drug is

    A. poisonous   B. habit-forming
    C. expensive   D. potent

15. While a growing health consciousness is apparent here and in many other countries, our knowledge of how to prevent and control disease far exceeds its application. This statement means MOST NEARLY that

    A. much of our knowledge of how to improve public health is not put into practice
    B. there has been little increase in our knowledge of disease prevention and control
    C. some of our knowledge on control of diseases is impossible to put into practice
    D. there has been no improvement in the prevention and control of disease

16. Developments in the field of nutrition have been an important part of medical progress. Not only have dietary cures been discovered for true nutritional diseases but, in almost every branch of medicine and surgery, therapy has been improved by more scientific methods of feeding. The one of the following which is the MOST accurate statement on the basis of the above paragraph is that

    A. nutrition plays a minor role in medicine
    B. dietary cures have therapeutic values only in cases of nutritional diseases
    C. proper nutrition is important in the cure of diseases in almost every branch of medicine
    D. nutritional diseases can be cured only by special diets

17. An individual may be wholly immune to one disease and ultra-susceptible to another; and such immunity, which may be born with the individual or acquired, has absolutely no relation to physique, robustness, or great vitality. The one of the following which is the MOST accurate statement on the basis of this paragraph is that

    A. an adult who is immune to a disease must have been immune to that disease as a child
    B. a person who is susceptible to one disease has a tendency to be susceptible to all diseases
    C. a person of poor physique and low vitality may nevertheless be immune to certain diseases
    D. persons of low vitality are more susceptible to diseases than persons of great vitality

18. If the doctor is in <u>consultation</u> with another doctor, he should not be disturbed.
    As used in this sentence, the word *consultation* means MOST NEARLY

    A. conference   B. operation   C. agreement   D. argument

19. A nurse should not <u>prescribe</u> for patients without the doctor's instructions.
    As used in this sentence, the word *prescribe* means MOST NEARLY

    A. explain the cuases of illness
    B. ascertain the case history
    C. determine the appointment time
    D. recommend treatment

20. The doctor has the right to <u>refer</u> patients to the hospital. As used in this sentence, the word *refer* means MOST NEARLY

    A. accept   B. admit   C. direct   D. accompany

21. An <u>antidote</u> is an agent which

    A. allays pain
    B. counteracts the effects of a poison
    C. reduces acidity
    D. stimulates the heart

22. Physical <u>therapy</u> has an important place in medicine. As used in this sentence, the word *therapy* means MOST NEARLY

    A. massage   B. treatment   C. exercise   D. examination

23. Doctors must not advertise or in any way solicit patients. As used in this sentence, the word *solicit* means MOST NEARLY

    A. actively seek
    B. greet
    C. exploit
    D. deliberately hurt

24. After examining the patient, the doctor indicated the prognosis of the illness. As used in this sentence, the word *prognosis* means MOST NEARLY

    A. probable course
    B. cause
    C. treatment
    D. past history

25. A doctor practicing *obstetrics* deals with

    A. glandular disorders
    B. deformities of the bones
    C. pregnancy
    D. children's diseases

26. The patient's condition was aggravated by a severe case of phobia. The word *phobia* means MOST NEARLY

    A. fever
    B. apathy
    C. indigestion
    D. fear

27. Neglect of immediate treatment may cause an illness to become chronic. The word *chronic* means MOST NEARLY

    A. incurable
    B. painful
    C. prolonged
    D. contagious

28. The one of the following which is NOT generally used to alleviate pain is

    A. aspirin   B. morphine   C. cocaine   D. quinine

29. The administration of a drug subcutaneously means administration by

    A. mouth
    B. injection beneath the skin
    C. application on the surface of the skin
    D. rectum

30. The one of the following which is NOT a disinfectant is

    A. boiling water
    B. iodine
    C. formaldehyde
    D. novocain

31. The one of the following which is LEAST related to the pulse rate of an individual is his

    A. blood pressure
    B. temperature
    C. weight
    D. emotional state

32. The one of the following which denotes normal vision is

    A. 20/10   B. 20/20   C. 20/30   D. 20/40

33. Of the following, the temperature which is MOST desirable for a babies' weighing room in a health center is _____ ° F.

    A. 60-62   B. 65-68   C. 75-77   D. 85-88

34. Of the following, it is MOST advisable for the operator to wear dark glasses during treatments by

    A. x-ray
    B. infrared radiation
    C. diathermy
    D. ultraviolet radiation

35. Of the following, the BEST method of sterilizing glassware for surgical purposes is by means of

    A. immersion in boiling water
    B. steaming under pressure
    C. cold sterilization
    D. washing thoroughly with soap and water

36. The apparatus used for sterilizing medical equipment by means of steam under pressure is the

    A. autoclave   B. manometer   C. catheter   D. reamer

37. After each use of a thermometer, it should be

    A. held under hot water for several minutes
    B. disinfected in a chemical solution
    C. rinsed in cold water
    D. wiped clean with cotton

38. The LEAST desirable action to take in administering first aid to a person suffering from shock is to

    A. give the patient some aromatic spirits of ammonia
    B. place the patient in a reclining position and elevate his legs
    C. loosen any tight clothing and place a pillow under his head
    D. place a hot water bottle near the patient's feet

39. Of the following symptoms, the one which does NOT generally accompany a fainting spell is

    A. a flushed face
    B. perspiration of the forehead
    C. shallow breathing
    D. a slow pulse

40. Assume that a six-year-old boy is brought to the clinic, bleeding profusely from a scalp wound. The doctor has not as yet arrived.
    Of the following, the MOST effective action for you to take is to

    A. wash the wound thoroughly with soap and water to prevent infection; apply pressure on the bleeding point; then treat for shock
    B. place the boy in a comfortable position; apply tincture of iodine to the wound to prevent infection; then treat for shock
    C. give the patient a stimulant; then attempt to stop the bleeding by applying digital pressure
    D. make the boy comfortable; place a compress over the wound and bandage snugly; then threat for shock

41. Of the following, the MOST frequently used method for the diagnosis of pulmonary tuberculosis is the

    A. blood test
    B. x-ray
    C. metabolism test
    D. urinalysis

42. Of the following conditions, the one which may be infectious is

    A. diabetes
    B. tuberculosis
    C. appendicitis
    D. hypertension

43. Of the following, observation of deviations from normal body weight may aid LEAST in determining the presence of

    A. glandular disturbances
    B. malnutrition
    C. organic disturbances
    D. mental deficiency

44. Leukemia is a disease of the blood characterized by a

    A. moderate increase in the red cell count and decrease in the white cell count
    B. marked decrease in the red cell count and an increase in the white cell count
    C. marked increase in the hemoglobin content
    D. marked decrease in the white cell count

45. The one of the following which is MOST commonly used in the treatment of arthritis is

    A. radium
    B. an electrocardiogram
    C. a radiograph
    D. diathermy

46. The fluoroscope is used CHIEFLY to

    A. provide a permanent picture of the condition of internal organs at a given time
    B. make a chart of the action of the muscles of the heart
    C. observe the internal structure and functioning of the organs of the body at a given time
    D. produce heat in the tissues of the body

47. A stethoscope is an instrument used for

    A. determining the blood pressure
    B. taking the body temperature
    C. chest examination
    D. determining the amount of sugar in the blood

48. The Dick test is used to determine susceptibility to
    A. measles B. scarlet fever
    C. diphtheria D. chickenpox

49. The aorta is a(n)
    A. bone B. artery C. ligament D. nerve

50. The esophagus is part of the
    A. alimentary canal B. abdominal wall
    C. mucous membrane D. circulatory system

51. Of the following, the one which is NOT a blood vessel is the
    A. vein B. capillary C. ganglion D. artery

52. Vital statistics include data reflating to
    A. births, deaths, and marriages
    B. the cost of food, clothing, and shelter
    C. the number of children per family unit
    D. diseases and their comparative mortality rates

53. In filing letters by subject, you should be MOST concerned with the
    A. name of the sender
    B. main topic of the letter
    C. date of the correspondence
    D. alphabetic cross reference

54. When arranging the record cards of patients in alphabetical order, the one of the following which should be filed THIRD is
    A. Charles A. Clarke B. James Clark
    C. Joan Carney D. Mae Cohen

55. The one of the following names which should be filed FIRST is
    A. Benjamin Dermody B. Frank Davidson
    C. Matthew Davids D. Seymour Diana

Questions 56-60.

DIRECTIONS: Questions 56 through 60 are to be answered on the basis of the chart below.

ATTENDANCE OF PATIENTS AT Y HEALTH CENTER
FOR WEEK OF APRIL 10

Clinic	Number Summoned for				Number Reported to			
	Baby	Chest	Eye	V.D.	Baby	Chest	Eye	V.D.
Monday	30	42	36	38	29	40	33	35
Tuesday	33	29	34	37	30	29	31	36
Wednesday	38	31	45	42	35	30	40	40
Thursday	41	48	41	32	36	45	39	28
Friday	35	37	39	36	33	35	37	32

56. On the basis of the above chart, it is CORRECT to say that 56.____

    A. more patients were summoned to the baby clinic than to the chest clinic during the week
    B. the same number of patients were absent from the eye clinic and the baby clinic during the week
    C. more patients reported to the eye clinic than to the chest clinic during the week
    D. more patients were summoned to the V.D. clinic than to the eye clinic during the week

57. On the basis of the above chart, the daily average number of patients summoned to the eye clinic exceeds the daily average reporting to the eye clinic by 57.____

    A. 3   B. 7   C. 11   D. 15

58. The percentage of all patients summoned to Y Health Center on Thursday who failed to report for their appointments is 58.____

    A. *less* than 5%
    B. *more* than 5% but less than 10%
    C. *more* than 10% but less than 15%
    D. *more* than 15%

59. The number of patients summoned for the entire week to the eye clinic exceeds the number of patients summoned to the baby clinic by 59.____

    A. 6   B. 9   C. 13   D. 18

60. The total number of patients who reported to Y Health Center for the week is 60.____

    A. 683   B. 693   C. 724   D. 744

Questions 61-80.

DIRECTIONS: Column I below lists words used in medical practice. Column II lists phrases which describe the words in Column I. In the space at the right, place the letter preceding the phrase in Column II which BEST describes the word in Column I.

COLUMN I	COLUMN II
61. Abrasion	A. A disturbance of digestion
62. Aseptic	B. Destroying the germs of disease
63. Cardiac	C. A general poisoning of the blood
64. Catarrh	D. An instrument used for injecting fluids
65. Contamination	E. A scraping off of the skin
66. Dermatology	F. Free from disease germs
67. Disinfectant	G. An apparatus for viewing internal organs by means of x-rays
68. Dyspepsia	H. An instrument for assisting the eye in observing minute objects
69. Epidemic	I. An inoculable immunizing agent
70. Epidermis	J. The extensive prevalence in a community of a disease
71. Incubation	K. Chemical product of an organ
72. Microscope	L. Preceding birth
73. Pediatrics	M. Fever
74. Plasma	N. The branch of medical science that relates to the skin and its diseases
75. Prenatal	O. Fluid part of the blood
76. Retina	P. The science of the hygienic care of children
77. Syphilis	Q. Infection by contact
78. Syringe	R. Relating to the heart
79. Toxemia	S. Inner structure of the eye
80. Vaccine	T. Outer portion of the skin
	U. Pertaining to the ductless gland
	V. An infectious venereal disease
	W. Pertaining to the hip
	X. The development of an infectious disease from the period of infection to that of the appearance of the first symptoms
	Y. Simple inflammation of a mucous membrane
	Z. An instrument for measuring blood pressure

KEY (CORRECT ANSWERS)

1. A	16. C	31. C	46. C	61. E	76. S
2. D	17. C	32. B	47. C	62. F	77. V
3. B	18. A	33. C	48. B	63. R	78. D
4. A	19. D	34. D	49. B	64. Y	79. C
5. C	20. C	35. B	50. A	65. Q	80. I
6. C	21. B	36. A	51. C	66. N	
7. C	22. B	37. B	52. A	67. B	
8. D	23. A	38. C	53. B	68. A	
9. D	24. A	39. A	54. A	69. J	
10. B	25. C	40. D	55. C	70. T	
11. C	26. D	41. B	56. C	71. X	
12. A	27. C	42. B	57. A	72. H	
13. B	28. D	43. D	58. B	73. P	
14. B	29. B	44. B	59. D	74. O	
15. A	30. D	45. D	60. B	75. L	

EXAMINATION SECTION
TEST 1

DIRECTIONS: Each question or incomplete statement is followed by several suggested answers or completions. Select the one that BEST answers the question or completes the statement. *PRINT THE LETTER OF THE CORRECT ANSWER IN THE SPACE AT THE RIGHT.*

1. Of the following, the MOST important reason for requiring that an employee have knowledge of medical office procedures is that

    A. she can take care of sick people in the absence of a doctor
    B. patients in the clinic will be impressed with her apparent knowledge
    C. she will be more helpful in her work at the clinic
    D. letters she may have to write will be more concise

    1.____

2. A newly appointed employee should have a good understanding of her functions in the Department of Health.
Of the following, the training which would be LEAST helpful to her in the performance of her functions is

    A. an understanding of the role of the Department of Health in the community
    B. development of skill in the technics of work in a health center
    C. information as to the services offered in the health center
    D. development of skill in the care of the sick in their own homes

    2.____

3. If an employee were called upon at the same time to attend to each of the following, the one she should do FIRST is

    A. sterilize instruments used in the examination of the last patient
    B. answer the telephone
    C. give the patient who is just leaving another appointment
    D. check to see if a patient who has just arrived has an appointment

    3.____

4. Of the following, the LEAST important reason for answering telephone calls promptly in the health clinic is that

    A. patients waiting in the clinic will be impressed with the self-importance of the employee
    B. patients calling for information will be answered quickly
    C. the public will get a favorable impression of the Department of Health
    D. it will result in better service by keeping the lines free for other calls

    4.____

5. Assume that the physician assigned to the clinic in which you work calls the clinic and tells you that he has been detained for half an hour and will not be able to report at 1:00 P.M. as scheduled.
You should

    A. not say anything about the call to anyone
    B. report this information to your immediate supervisor
    C. tell the patient scheduled for 1:00 P.M. to come back the next day
    D. tell the physician that he must come at 1:00 P.M. since a patient has been scheduled for that time

    5.____

2 (#1)

6. Assume that a physician who is examining a patient asks you to hand him a certain instrument from the tray. You do not know exactly what he is referring to.
   The BEST thing for you to do is to

   A. give him an instrument which you think might be suitable for the examination
   B. ask him to repeat what he said
   C. admit that you cannot identify the instrument he wants
   D. tell him that there is no such instrument on the tray

7. Assume that a patient asks you to explain something the doctor told her about her illness which she says she does not understand.
   For you to suggest that she tell the doctor that she did not understand what he told her and ask him to explain it again is

   A. *advisable;* the patient will be impressed by your interest in her
   B. *inadvisable;* patients get tired of the run-around
   C. *advisable;* the doctor is best qualified to answer questions concerning or affecting the patient's health
   D. *inadvisable;* the patient will lose confidence in your ability

8. Assume that, after you have been employed for several months, the nurse who is your immediate supervisor summons you to her office. She tells you that she has noticed on several occasions that you have been careless about
   your personal appearance. In this instance, it would be

   A. proper for you to tell her that your personal appearance is no concern of hers
   B. advisable for you to listen politely to her and then do nothing about it
   C. fitting for you to tell her that the other employees in the clinic are just as careless
   D. best for you to thank her for her interest and to tell her that you will make an effort to be more careful

9. One of the patients at the Health Center insists that she be sent to a different doctor as she does not like the doctor she saw last week.
   Of the following answers, the one that is MOST advisable for you to give to the patient is that

   A. she will have to take whatever doctor is available
   B. all the clinic doctors are equally good
   C. you will try to send her to another doctor
   D. she should see the nurse in charge

10. Suppose that the doctor in the clinic has given you an order which is contrary to the usual clinic procedure. Of the following, the BEST action for you to take is to

    A. point out to the doctor the usual clinic procedure and then do as he tells you
    B. refuse to do what he tells you as it is contrary to the usual procedure
    C. refuse to do what he tells you and call the nurse in charge
    D. do as the doctor tells you and at the first opportunity report the occurrence to the nurse in charge

11. When filing some patients' record cards in an alphabetic file, you notice that one card obviously has been misfiled.
    In this case, it would be MOST advisable for you to

    A. pay no attention to this as you believe it was not your error
    B. pull out the card and file it correctly
    C. report this to the clinic supervisor and suggest to her that she reprimand the employee who you believe is responsible for the misfiling
    D. take no particular care in the future when filing cards since errors will occur anyway

12. Assume that you are working directly with children in a well baby clinic. You feel feverish.
    Of the following, the BEST action for you to take is to

    A. wait and see whether you feel better; you don't want to seem to be a chronic complainer
    B. report immediately to the nurse in charge that you do not feel well
    C. take your temperature and, if it is over 101° F, report to the nurse in charge
    D. report to the nurse in charge only if you have other symptoms

13. As a receptionist in a public health center, you have certain responsibilities towards patients and other callers. You should greet each caller promptly and courteously. Never keep a caller waiting while you carry on a personal conversation, either on the telephone or with another employee. However, if you are occupied with clinic matters, give the caller to understand that you will be with him in a short while.
    On the basis of this paragraph, if a caller comes in while you are discussing with the nurse in charge coverage of the clinic during the lunch hour, the one of the following actions which would be the BEST for you to take is to

    A. stop and take care of his needs immediately as you should never keep a caller waiting
    B. nod to him and continue making plans for clinic coverage
    C. say to him that you will take care of him in a moment; then finish making your plans for clinic coverage
    D. finish making plans for clinic coverage with the nurse in charge and then inquire into the caller's needs

14. Assume that you are responsible for scheduling clinic appointments. One of the patients who has to report to the clinic every Tuesday morning asks that his appointments be scheduled for the last half hour of the clinic session. It has been the practice in this clinic to keep the last half hour open only for emergency appointments, and to schedule all appointments in order, from the time when the clinic opens.
    Of the following, the BEST action for you to take is to

    A. schedule the appointment at the time requested by the patient as he probably has a good reason for wanting it then
    B. disregard his request as no one attending a clinic should be given special consideration
    C. deny his request unless he has a medical reason for asking for a late appointment
    D. refer the request to the nurse in charge to determine if he should be given a late appointment

15. Suppose that a patient who is registered in the Social Hygiene Clinic of a Health Center appears in a drunken condition for a scheduled appointment.
    Of the following, the BEST action for you to take is to

    A. inform the nurse in charge of the situation
    B. have him await his turn with the other patients
    C. send him home, telling him not to return until he is sober
    D. arrange for him to see the doctor immediately

16. Assume that you have been asked by your supervisor to instruct a newly-appointed aide in the performance of a given task.
    Of the following, the BEST procedure for you to follow is

    A. to check her work only once after you have shown her how to do it; continued supervision after this should be the supervisor's responsibility
    B. not to check her work after you have shown her how to do it as she may resent your supervision
    C. not to check her work immediately but wait until she has done the task several times in order to give her a fair chance
    D. to check her work at frequent intervals after you have shown her how to do it until she is able to perform the given task

17. A worker should be carefully introduced to the clinic to which she has been assigned. The period of orientation will vary widely with the individual, her previous experience, and the type of clinic to which she is assigned.
    In general, it will include an introduction to the physical set-up, the personnel, the type of service to be rendered, and the ideals of the clinic. In the beginning, the new worker should be given simple assignments and close supervision. The program should be arranged so as to give the nurse in charge opportunity to study the worker as to personality, general ability, or any special handicaps.
    According to this paragraph, the one of the following statements that is MOST accurate is that, during the first few days, the new worker should

    A. do nothing but observe the physical set-up, the personnel, the type of service rendered, the ideals of the clinic
    B. be given a 30 hour course in the clinic to which she is assigned, including the physical set-up, the personnel, the ideals of the clinic
    C. be observed by the nurse in charge as to her ability to do the work in the clinic to which she has been assigned
    D. be closely supervised by the nurse in charge until she has a thorough knowledge of the clinic

18. Preparing a patient for physical examination has important mental aspects. Because each patient is individual in his reactions, a worker must plan her approach so as to deal with these reactions sympathetically. Thus, one patient may be afraid of the pain an examination may cause him immediately, another may fear that he will have unpleasant effects later, and still another may be only curious about the examination and have neither fear nor anxiety.
    On the basis of this paragraph, the one of the following statements that BEST describes the reactions of patients when undergoing examination is that all patients

    A. are afraid when being examined
    B. react differently to an examination
    C. are afraid of the after-effects of an examination
    D. are curious about the examination

19. A recently published article states: Weight for height and age is, as many have previously held, an inadequate index of the *nutritional status* of a child. It is unscientific and unfair to set average weight as a goal for all children or for an individual child. Weighing and measuring, however, should be continued as a record of the trend of individual growth which is of value to the physician in relation to other findings and as valuable devices to interest the child in his growth.
According to this article, weighing and measuring the height of children

   A. are of no value and should be stopped
   B. are useful to the physician
   C. are of no value but give interesting information
   D. indicate the nutritional status of the child

19.____

20. Blood pressure is the force that the blood exerts against the walls of the vessels through which it flows. The blood pressure is commonly meant to be the pressure in the arteries. The pressure in the arteries varies with the contraction (work period) and the relaxation (rest period) of the heart. When the heart contracts, the blood in the arteries is at its greatest pressure. This is called the systolic pressure. When the heart relaxes, the blood in the arteries is at its lowest pressure. This is called the diastolic pressure. The difference between both pressures is called the pulse pressure.
The one of the following statements that is MOST accurate on the basis of this paragraph is that

   A. the blood in the arteries is at its greatest pressure during contraction
   B. systolic pressure measures the blood in the arteries when the heart is relaxed
   C. blood pressure is determined by obtaining the difference between systolic and diastolic pressure
   D. pulse pressure is the same as blood pressure

20.____

21. Lymph is a clear fluid, rich in white blood cells, and is actually blood plasma which has filtered through the walls of capillaries. It is circulated through the lymph vessels and in all the tissue spaces of the body. It carries nourishment and oxygen to the tissues and waste products away from them.
The one of the following statements that is NOT correct on the basis of this paragraph is that lymph

   A. contains red blood cells
   B. contains white blood cells
   C. is a basic part of blood
   D. is circulated through the body

21.____

22. When storing medical supplies, it is important to remember that liquids should be labeled

   A. only if the liquids are poisonous and there is the slightest chance that they will not be recognized
   B. whenever there is the slightest chance that they will not be recognized
   C. at all times, and discarded if labels have become detached
   D. only in those cases where the liquids will be given to patients

22.____

23. When dusting metal countertops in the clinic, it is BEST to use a clean cloth which is

   A. medicated   B. wet   C. dry   D. damp

23.____

24. Of the following statements concerning a hypodermic syringe, the one that is MOST correct is that a plunger 24.____

   A. used for taking blood specimens can be used with any syringe barrel
   B. can be used for any syringe barrel as long as it goes in easily
   C. can be used only with the syringe barrel that was made for it
   D. must be used with the syringe barrel that was made for it only if it is to be used for injections

25. The one of the following which should NOT be done when using a thermometer is to 25.____

   A. shake down the thermometer to 95F before taking the patient's temperature
   B. ask the patient to keep his lips closed when taking the temperature orally
   C. wash the thermometer in hot soapy water after use
   D. keep the thermometer in a container of alcohol when not in use

26. The temperature of an adult when taken by rectum is usually _____ than if taken _____ under the armpit. 26.____

   A. *higher;* either by mouth or
   B. *higher;* by mouth and lower than if taken
   C. *lower;* either by mouth or
   D. *lower;* by mouth and higher if taken

27. Of the following tests, the one which is associated with tuberculosis is the _____ test. 27.____

   A. Schick   B. Mantoux   C. Dick   D. Kahn

28. A needle that has been used to draw blood should be rinsed immediately after use in 28.____

   A. a disinfectant solution   B. hot water
   C. cold water   D. hot, soapy water

29. Of the following, the statement that is MOST correct is that a hypodermic needle should be checked for burrs, hooks, and sharpness 29.____

   A. once a week
   B. before it is sterilized
   C. after it has been sterilized
   D. after it has been used three or four times

30. The MOST accurate of the following statements is that, when a syringe and needle are being sterilized by boiling, the 30.____

   A. plunger must be completely out of the barrel
   B. needle should be left attached to the barrel as when in use
   C. plunger may be completely inside the barrel
   D. needle should be boiled at least twice as long as the syringe

31. Of the following, the MOST important reason for washing an instrument in hot soapy water is to 31.____

   A. sterilize the instrument
   B. destroy germs by heat
   C. destroy germs by coagulation
   D. remove foreign matter and bacteria

32. Assume that a hypodermic needle which is to be used for injection is accidentally brushed at the tip by your hand. Of the following, the action which should be taken before this needle is used is that it be

    A. washed under the hot water tap
    B. wiped with a sterile piece of gauze
    C. washed in hot soapy water, then rinsed in sterile water
    D. boiled for ten minutes

33. The CORRECT way to sterilize a scalpel is to

    A. place it in a chemical germicide
    B. boil it for 10 minutes
    C. put it in the autoclave
    D. pass it through a bright flame

34. Assume that a tray of instruments has been accidentally left uncovered for five minutes after it had been sterilized.
    Of the following, the action you should take to ensure that the instruments are sterile for use is to

    A. dip them in boiling water
    B. boil them for 10 minutes
    C. replace the cover on the tray
    D. wipe each instrument with sterile gauze

35. An intramuscular injection is MOST likely to be used in the administration of

    A. smallpox vaccine
    B. streptomycin
    C. glucose
    D. blood

36. The one of the following which is NOT a normal element of blood is

    A. hemoglobin
    B. a leucocyte
    C. marrow
    D. a platelet

37. Of the following statements regarding the Salk vaccine, the MOST accurate one is that it

    A. immunizes children and adults against paralytic poliomyelitis
    B. is a test to determine the presence of poliomyelitis virus in the blood
    C. is a test to determine whether a child is immune to poliomyelitis
    D. is used in the treatment of patients suffering from paralytic poliomyelitis

38. The GREATEST success in the treatment of cancer has been in cancer of the

    A. blood   B. stomach   C. liver   D. skin

39. An autopsy is a(n)

    A. type of blood test
    B. examination of tissue removed from a living organism
    C. examination of a human body after death
    D. test to determine the acidity of body fluids

40. The word *vascular* is MOST closely associated with

   A. the circulatory system
   B. respiration
   C. digestion
   D. the nervous system

41. The word *diagnosis* means MOST NEARLY

   A. preparation of a diagram
   B. determination of an illness
   C. medical examination of a patient
   D. written prescription

42. A tendon connects

   A. bone to bone
   B. muscle to bone
   C. muscle to muscle
   D. muscle to ligament

43. Blood takes on oxygen as it passes through the

   A. liver   B. heart   C. spleen   D. lungs

44. The fatty substance in the blood which is deposited in the artery walls and which is believed to cause hardening of the arteries is called

   A. amino acid   B. phenol   C. cholesterol   D. pectin

45. The digestive canal includes the

   A. stomach, small intestine, large intestine, and rectum
   B. stomach, larynx, large intestine, and rectum
   C. trachea, small intestine, large intestine, and rectum
   D. stomach, small intestine, large intestine, and abdominal cavity

46. When giving artificial respiration, it should be kept in mind that air is drawn into the lungs by the

   A. expansion of the chest cavity
   B. contraction of the chest cavity
   C. expansion of the lungs
   D. contraction of the lungs

47. The formula for converting degrees Centigrade to degrees Fahrenheit is as follows:
   Fahrenheit = 9/5 of Centigrade + 32°, or
   (multiply the number of degrees Centigrade by 9, divide by 5 and add 32)

   If the Centigrade thermometer reads 25°, the temperature, in degrees Fahrenheit, is

   A. 13   B. 45   C. 53   D. 77

48. To make a certain preparation, you have been told to mix one ounce of Liquid A and 3 ounces of Liquid B.
    If you have used 18 ounces of Liquid B in preparing a larger amount, the number of ounces of Liquid A you should use is

    A. 6   B. 15   C. 21   D. 54

49. If one inch is equal to approximately 2.5 centimeters, the number of inches in fifteen centimeters is MOST NEARLY

    A. 1.6   B. 6   C. 12.5   D. 37.5

Questions 50-52.

DIRECTIONS: Questions 50 through 52 are to be answered on the basis of the following situation.

you have been asked to keep records of the time spent with each patient by the doctors in the clinic where you are assigned, Iour notes show that Dr. Jones spent the following amount of time with each patient he examined on a certain day:

    Patient A - 14 minutes;   Patient B - 13 minutes;
    Patient C - 34 minutes;   Patient D - 48 minutes;
    Patient E - 26 minutes;   Patient F - 20 minutes;
    Patient G - 25 minutes.

50. The average number of minutes spent by Dr. Jones with each patient is MOST NEARLY

    A. 20   B. 25   C. 30   D. 35

51. If Dr. Jones is to take care of the seven patients mentioned above at one session, the number of hours he will have to remain at the clinic is MOST NEARLY _____ hour(s).

    A. 1   B. 2   C. 3   D. 4

52. The one of the following groups of patients that required the LEAST time to be examined is Patients

    A. A, C, and E   B. B, D, and F
    C. C, E, and G   D. A, D, and G

Questions 53-60.

DIRECTIONS: Questions 53 through 60 are to be answered on the basis of the usual rules of filing. Column I lists the names of 8 clinic patients. Column II lists the headings of file drawers into which you are to place the records of these patients. In the space at the right, corresponding to the names in Column I, print the letter preceding the heading of the file drawer in which the record should be filed.

COLUMN I

53. Thomas Adams
54. Joseph Albert
55. Frank Anaster
56. Charles Abt
57. John Alfred
58. Louis Aron
59. Francis Amos
60. William Adler

COLUMN II

A. Aab-Abi
B. Abj-Ach
C. Aci-Aco
D. Acp-Ada
E. Adb-Afr
F. Afs-Ago
G. Agp-Ahz
H. Aia-Ako
I. Akp-Ald
J. Ale-Amo
K. Amp-Aor
L. Aos-Apr
M. Aps-Asi
N. Asj-Ati
O. Atj-Awz

53. _____
54. _____
55. _____
56. _____
57. _____
58. _____
59. _____
60. _____

KEY (CORRECT ANSWERS)

1.	C	16.	D	31.	D	46.	A
2.	D	17.	C	32.	D	47.	D
3.	B	18.	B	33.	A	48.	A
4.	A	19.	B	34.	B	49.	B
5.	B	20.	A	35.	B	50.	B
6.	C	21.	A	36.	C	51.	C
7.	C	22.	C	37.	A	52.	A
8.	D	23.	D	38.	D	53.	D
9.	D	24.	C	39.	C	54.	I
10.	A	25.	C	40.	A	55.	K
11.	B	26.	A	41.	B	56.	B
12.	B	27.	B	42.	B	57.	J
13.	C	28.	C	43.	D	58.	M
14.	D	29.	B	44.	C	59.	J
15.	A	30.	A	45.	A	60.	E

TEST 2

DIRECTIONS: Each question or incomplete statement is followed by several suggested answers or completions. Select the one that BEST answers the question or completes the statement. *PRINT THE LETTER OF THE CORRECT ANSWER IN THE SPACE AT THE RIGHT.*

Questions 1-6.

DIRECTIONS: In answering Questions 1 through 6, alphabetize the four names listed in each question; then print in the space at the right the four letters preceding the alphabetized names to show the CORRECT alphabetical arrangement of the four names.

1. A. Frank Adam B. Frank Aarons 1._____
   C. Frank Aaron D. Frank Adams

2. A. Richard Lavine B. Richard Levine 2._____
   C. Edward Lawrence D. Edward Loraine

3. A. G. Frank Adam B. Frank Adam 3._____
   C. Fanny Adam D. Franklin Adam

4. A. George Cohn B. Richard Cohen 4._____
   C. Thomas Cohane D. George Cohan

5. A. Paul Shultz B. Robert Schmid 5._____
   C. Joseph Schwartz D. Edward Schmidt

6. A. Peter Consilazio B. Frank Consolezio 6._____
   C. Robert Consalizio D. Ella Consolizio

Questions 7-13.

DIRECTIONS: For Questions 7 through 13, select the letter preceding the word which means MOST NEARLY the same as the word in capital letters.

7. LEGIBLE 7._____

   A. readable   B. eligible   C. learned   D. lawful

8. OBSERVE 8._____

   A. assist   B. watch   C. correct   D. oppose

9. HABITUAL 9._____

   A. punctual   B. occasional
   C. usual   D. actual

10. CHRONOLOGICAL 10._____

    A. successive   B. earlier
    C. later   D. studious

11. ARREST

    A. punish   B. run   C. threaten   D. stop

11.____

12. ABSTAIN

    A. refrain   B. indulge   C. discolor   D. spoil

12.____

13. TOXIC

    A. poisonous   B. decaying
    C. taxing   D. defective

13.____

14. TOLERATE

    A. fear   B. forgive   C. allow   D. despise

14.____

15. VENTILATE

    A. vacate   B. air   C. extricate   D. heat

15.____

16. SUPERIOR

    A. perfect   B. subordinate
    C. lower   D. higher

16.____

17. EXTREMITY

    A. extent   B. limb   C. illness   D. execution

17.____

18. DIVULGED

    A. unrefined   B. secreted
    C. revealed   D. divided

18.____

19. SIPHON

    A. drain   B. drink   C. compute   D. discard

19.____

20. EXPIRATION

    A. trip   B. demonstration
    C. examination   D. end

20.____

Questions 21-40.

DIRECTIONS: Column I lists 20 words, numbered 21 through 40, which are used in medical practice. Column II lists words or phrases which describe the words in Column I. In the space at the right, next to the number of each of the words in Column I, place the letter preceding the words or phrases in Column II which BEST describes the word in Column I.

COLUMN I	COLUMN II
21. Anemia	A. A tube used to drain fluid from the bladder
22. Anesthetic	B. The skull
23. Arthritis	C. Inflammation of a joint
24. Aseptic	D. A fluid injected into the rectum for the purpose of clearing out the bowels
25. Astigmatism	E. A drug used in surgery which makes one insensible to pain
26. Catheter	F. Rheumatic pain in the back
27. Cranium	G. The branch of medicine concerned with diseases of the eye
28. Diathermy	H. Examination of the inner parts of the body by use of x-rays and a special screen
29. Enema	I. free from disease germs
30. Electrocardiograph	J. Deficiency of blood
31. Forceps	K. The branch of medicine concerned with diseases of women
32. Gynecology	L. A tumorous growth
33. Lesion	M. A structural defect of the eye
34. Lumbago	N. An apparatus for sterilization under pressurized steam
35. Microscope	O. The shoulder blade
36. Obstetrics	P. A type of treatment which depends upon production of heat in the tissues by high frequency current
37. Ophthalmology	Q. An instrument for recording electric changes caused by contraction of the muscles of the heart
38. Postnatal	R. An instrument for magnifying minute organisms
39. Rabies	S. The branch of medicine concerned with the care and delivery of pregnant women
40. Stethoscope	T. A wound or injury
	U. An acute infectious disease which is transmitted by the bite of dogs and other animals
	V. A band of tissue which connects bones or holds organs in place
	W. A medication used to calm nerves
	X. An instrument used to listen to sounds in the heart
	Y. A pair of tongs
	Z. Occurring after birth

21. ____
22. ____
23. ____
24. ____
25. ____
26. ____
27. ____
28. ____
29. ____
30. ____
31. ____
32. ____
33. ____
34. ____
35. ____
36. ____
37. ____
38. ____
39. ____
40. ____

KEY (CORRECT ANSWERS)

1.	C,B,A,D	11.	D	21.	J	31.	Y
2.	A,C,B,D	12.	A	22.	E	32.	K
3.	C,B,D,A	13.	A	23.	C	33.	T
4.	D,C,B,A	14.	C	24.	I	34.	F
5.	B,D,C,A	15.	B	25.	M	35.	R
6.	C,A,B,D	16.	D	26.	A	36.	S
7.	A	17.	B	27.	B	37.	G
8.	B	18.	C	28.	P	38.	Z
9.	C	19.	A	29.	D	39.	U
10.	A	20.	D	30.	Q	40.	X

EXAMINATION SECTION
TEST 1

DIRECTIONS: Each question or incomplete statement is followed by several suggested answers or completions. Select the one that BEST answers the question or completes the statement. *PRINT THE LETTER OF THE CORRECT ANSWER IN THE SPACE AT THE RIGHT.*

1. An employee should know not only the details of his own job but the main objective of the organization for which he works.
   The MAIN objective of a health center may BEST be described as the

   A. orderly and efficient management of the health center
   B. improvement of the health of the community it serves
   C. courteous treatment of patients who are poor
   D. enforcement of the health laws of the city

   1._____

2. The MOST appropriate of the following statements for Miss Smith, who works in the cardiac clinic, to make when answering the clinic telephone is:

   A. This is the Cardiac Clinic. Who's calling please?
   B. Hello. This is Miss Smith.
   C. Cardiac Clinic, Miss Smith speaking. May I help you?
   D. Miss Smith speaking. To whom do you wish to speak?

   2._____

3. Of the following, the CHIEF reason why you should be familiar with medical terminology is so that you can

   A. be of greatest assistance to the doctors and nurses
   B. answer the patient's questions about their symptoms and treatments
   C. know what supplies to order for the clinic
   D. understand the medical publications which are sent to the clinic

   3._____

4. Assume that instructions have been issued in your clinic that medical information is not to be given to patients. Of the following, the BEST reason for this policy is that

   A. the relationship between the clinic staff and clinic patients, although friendly, should remain impersonal
   B. the health of a patient is a private matter which should not be discussed in public
   C. incorrect medical information might be given to the patient
   D. only the nurse in charge should be permitted to give medical information to patients

   4._____

5. Of the following, the BEST reason for keeping clinic records confidential is to

   A. protect the patient who may not want others to know certain information
   B. protect the health station in case errors have been made
   C. prevent publicity about the health station which may keep patients from coming to the clinics
   D. avoid the extra work involved in giving out information

   5._____

6. To give each patient who is to return to the clinic a card with the date of his next appointment written on it is

   6._____

A. unnecessary; it is sufficient to tell him when to come back
B. of little value; some of the patients may not be able to read English
C. impractical; too much time would be taken up in writing the cards
D. good practice; the patient would be less likely to forget his next date

7. When setting up a *tickler* file for patients' appointments in your clinic, you should arrange the cards according to the

    A. name of the patient
    B. date when the patient is due in the clinic
    C. condition for which the patient is being treated
    D. name of the doctor

8. Assume that you are responsible for maintaining the patients' record file in the clinic to which you are assigned. Frequently, the other clinics in the health center where you work borrow record cards from your clinic files.
The BEST way for you to avoid difficulty in locating cards which may have been borrowed by other clinics is to

    A. make out a duplicate card for any clinic that wishes to borrow a card from your file
    B. refuse to lend your card to any other clinic unless the other clinic's personnel officer promises to return the card in person
    C. report it to your supervisor if anyone fails to return a card after a reasonable time
    D. have the person who borrows a card fill out an out-of-file card and place it in the file whenever a record card is removed

9. Suppose that you are given an unalphabetized list of 500 clinic patients and a set of unalphabetized record cards. Your supervisor asks you to determine if there is a record card for each patient whose name is on the list.
For you to first arrange the record cards in alphabetical order before checking them with the names on the list is

    A. *desirable;* this will make it easier to check each name on the list against the patients' record cards
    B. *undesirable;* it is just as easy to alphabetize the names on the list as it is to rearrange the record cards
    C. *desirable;* this extra work with the record cards will give you more information about the patients
    D. *undesirable;* adding an extra step to the procedure makes the work too complicated

10. Suppose that you have been given about two thousand 3x5 cards to arrange in numerical order.
For you to sort the cards into broad groups, such as 1-100, 101-200, etc., and then arrange each group of cards in numerical order is

    A. *desirable;* you will not be so apt to lose your place if interrupted when working with small groups of cards
    B. *undesirable;* setting up a large number of groups of cards leads to more errors
    C. *desirable;* the work can be done more quickly and easily with smaller groups of cards than with the entire group at once
    D. *undesirable;* any procedure which requires so many steps wastes too much time

11. Of the following, the MOST important reason for keeping accurate records of clinic patients is that

    A. these records provide valuable information for medical research purposes
    B. accurate records are necessary to provide satisfactory medical care for the patients on return visits
    C. complete records are necessary in order to prepare accurate and complete statistical reports on the work of the clinic
    D. these records will show the large amount of work performed in the clinic

12. Suppose that one of the doctors who has been seeing patients on Wednesday changes his clinic day to Thursday. Two women who have previously had Wednesday appointments ask to come in on Thursday because they have great confidence in this doctor. For you to try to make Thursday appointments for them would be

    A. *correct;* the wishes of the patients should be considered in making appointments
    B. *wrong;* if the request were granted, the other patients would also want to have their appointments changed
    C. *correct;* most patients would rather come to the clinic on Wednesdays
    D. *wrong;* patients should not become too dependent upon any one physician

13. Of the following, the CHIEF reason for paying attention to a complaint from a clinic patient is that

    A. government employees should always be courteous to the public
    B. most people like to have others pay attention to their complaints
    C. it does no harm to listen to complaints even if there is no merit to them
    D. the patient may have good reason to complain

14. Assume that it is the rule in the clinic that the doctor is to sign the personal record card of each patient he examines. While you are filing the patients' record cards after the doctor has left the clinic, you notice that he has not signed the card of one of the patients he examined. Of the following, the MOST appropriate action for you to take is to

    A. sign your own name on the card since the doctor has left the clinic
    B. write the doctor's name on the card and sign your initials
    C. file the unsigned card in the record file with the other cards
    D. hold the card out and return it to the doctor for his signature on his next visit

15. Assume that it is the rule in the clinic that no patient may be seen after 4:00 P.M. so that the physicians and nurses will have time to write up cases and prepare for the following day. A few minutes after 4:00 P.M., an old woman who says she is in great pain and discomfort appears and asks for a doctor.
    For you to try to arrange for a physician to see her is

    A. *proper;* other patients waiting in the clinic will see how kind you are to sick people
    B. *improper;* a rule should never be broken by public health personnel
    C. *proper;* rules should not be interpreted too strictly when dealing with sick people
    D. *improper;* the physician would be very annoyed if you disturbed him after 4:00 P.M.

16. Assume that you have been instructed to note on the record of each child who is vaccinated the lot number of the vaccine used.
    Of the following, the MOST probable reason for this instruction is so that

A. a record can be kept of how much vaccine is used every year
B. if the child has an unfavorable reaction, the lot may be tested to determine the reason
C. no child will receive more than one vaccination
D. the oldest vaccine will be used first

17. The mother of a young child who is to be vaccinated against smallpox informs you that he gets hysterical at the sight of a needle.
Of the following, the BEST thing for you to do is to

   A. assure the mother that the child's fears are groundless
   B. speak to the child about the need to be protected against a serious disease like smallpox
   C. tell the head nurse about the child's fear before he is called for vaccination
   D. promise the child a lollypop or toy if he behaves and does not cry

18. A 10-year-old boy who is grossly overweight refuses to remove any of his clothing before being weighed, apparently because of embarrassment.
Of the following, it is BEST for you to

   A. weigh him fully dressed and note this fact on the record
   B. insist that he remove his clothing since otherwise the record would be inaccurate
   C. note on the record card *grossly overweight,* as you cannot weigh him with his clothing
   D. ask the head nurse to use her authority to make the boy undress

19. You notice that an 8-year-old boy who attends the clinic stammers badly.
Of the following, it is BEST for you to

   A. tell the doctor about his stammering in the boy's presence
   B. tell the boy each time you see him that his speech has improved
   C. ask the boy if he would like to go to a speech correction clinic
   D. make no reference to his stammer in the boy's presence

20. Of the following, the MOST important reason why you should remain with a 4-year-old child when his temperature is being taken by mouth is that otherwise the child might

   A. fall off the chair and fracture an arm or leg
   B. break the thermometer while it is in his mouth
   C. remove the thermometer from his mouth and misplace it
   D. leave the examining room and return to his mother

21. The BEST way to take the temperature of an infant is by

   A. feeling his forehead
   B. using an oral thermometer
   C. placing a thermometer under his armpit
   D. using a rectal thermometer

22. When the temperature of an adult is taken rectally, it is LEAST accurate to say that the

   A. temperature reading will be higher than if it were taken orally
   B. thermometer should be lubricated before use

C. thermometer should be in place for at least ten minutes
D. temperature reading is likely to be more accurate than if it were taken orally

23. When the temperature of an adult is taken orally, it is LEAST accurate to say that the   23.____

   A. thermometer should be washed with alcohol before it is used
   B. thermometer should be taken down below 96° F before it is used
   C. patient's temperature may be taken immediately after he has smoked a cigarette
   D. patient should be inactive just before his temperature is taken

24. The nurse described the test to the patient before bringing him to the examining room for   24.____
    a basal metabolism test.
    Her action may BEST be described as

   A. *correat;* the patient will be more cooperative if he knows what to expect
   B. *wrong;* the nurse does not know how the test will affect the patient
   C. *correct;* the nurse can judge whether the patient is too upset by this information to take the test
   D. *wrong;* explaining the test beforehand will only make the patient nervous

25. When a patient's sputum test is *positive,* it means that the   25.____

   A. patient's sputum is plentiful
   B. doctor has made an accurate diagnosis
   C. patient has recovered and is now in good health
   D. laboratory reports that the patient's sputum contains certain disease germs

26. A biopsy can BEST be described as a(n)   26.____

   A. pre-cancerous condition   B. examination of tissues
   C. living organism   D. germicidal solution

27. The *scratch* or *patch* test is usually given when testing for   27.____

   A. allergies   B. rheumatic fever
   C. blood poisoning   D. diabetes

28. Gamma globulin is frequently given to children after exposure to and before the appear-   28.____
    ance of symptoms of

   A. measles   B. smallpox
   C. tetanus   D. chickenpox

29. Of the following, the one which is NOT a respiratory disease is   29.____

   A. bronchitis   B. pneumonia
   C. nephritis   D. croup

30. A physician who specializes in the treatment of conditions affecting the skin is known as   30.____
    a

   A. urologist   B. dermatologist
   C. toxicologist   D. ophthalmologist

31. The branch of medicine which deals with diseases peculiar to women is

   A. pathology
   B. orthopedics
   C. neurology
   D. gynecology

32. The branch of medicine which deals with diseases of old age is called

   A. pediatrics
   B. geriatrics
   C. serology
   D. histology

33. *Petit mal* is a form of

   A. epilepsy
   B. syphilis
   C. diabetes
   D. malaria

34. Glaucoma is a disease of the

   A. thyroid gland
   B. liver
   C. bladder
   D. eye

35. A patient who has edema has

   A. not enough red blood cells
   B. too much water in the body tissues
   C. blood in the urine
   D. a swollen gland

36. The thoracic area of the body is located in the

   A. abdomen
   B. lower back
   C. chest
   D. neck

37. An electrocardiograph is MOST usually used in examination of the

   A. brain
   B. heart
   C. kidney
   D. gall bladder

38. The word *coagulate* means MOST NEARLY to

   A. bleed excessively
   B. break up
   C. work together
   D. form a clot

39. A stethoscope is used to examine the patient's

   A. heart
   B. patellar reflex
   C. blood cells
   D. spinal fluid

40. A pelvimeter is MOST usually used in the examination of a patient in the _____ clinic.

   A. chest   B. cancer   C. prenatal   D. eye

41. Tuberculin may BEST be described as a

   A. virus infection of the lungs
   B. preparation used in the diagnosis of tuberculosis
   C. sanitarium for tuberculous patients
   D. form of cancer of the lung

42. An autoclave is a(n)

    A. automatic dispenser of instruments needed for clinic examinations
    B. sterile place for storing clinic supplies until they are needed
    C. apparatus for sterilizing equipment under steam pressure
    D. portable self-operating general anesthesia unit

43. Radiation therapy is

    A. the recording of electrical impulses of the body on a graph
    B. a study of the effects of radiation fall-out on the human body
    C. a form of treatment used for certain diseases
    D. the filming of internal parts of the body through the use of x-rays

44. Diathermy is the treatment of patients by

    A. scientific use of baths and mineral waters
    B. insertion of radium into diseased tissues
    C. intravenous feedings of vitamins and minerals
    D. electrical generation of heat in the body tissues

45. The measurement of blood pressure involves two readings, which are known as _____ and _____.

    A. metabolic; diastolic   B. systolic; diastolic
    C. metabolic; hyperbolic   D. hyperbolic; systolic

46. The Snellen chart is used in examinations of the

    A. eyes   B. blood   C. urine   D. bile

47. An enema is MOST generally used to

    A. induce vomiting   B. irrigate the stomach
    C. clear the bowels   D. drain the urinary bladder

48. A bronchoscope is usually used in examinations of the

    A. kidneys   B. heart   C. stomach   D. lungs

49. The Wassermann test is used to find out if a patient has

    A. diphtheria   B. leukemia
    C. scarlet fever   D. syphilis

50. If a boiling water sterilizer is used, the minimum time necessary to sterilize instruments is MOST NEARLY _____ hour(s).

    A. 1/2   B. 1   C. 1 1/2   D. 2

KEY (CORRECT ANSWERS)

1. B	11. B	21. D	31. D	41. B
2. C	12. A	22. C	32. B	42. C
3. A	13. D	23. C	33. A	43. C
4. C	14. D	24. A	34. D	44. D
5. A	15. C	25. D	35. B	45. B
6. D	16. B	26. B	36. C	46. A
7. B	17. C	27. A	37. B	47. C
8. D	18. A	28. A	38. D	48. D
9. A	19. D	29. C	39. A	49. D
10. C	20. B	30. B	40. C	50. A

TEST 2

DIRECTIONS: Each question or incomplete statement is followed by several suggested answers or completions. Select the one that BEST answers the question or completes the statement. *PRINT THE LETTER OF THE CORRECT ANSWER IN THE SPACE AT THE RIGHT.*

1. To sterilize towels and dry gauze dressings in the health clinic, it is MOST advisable to   1.____

    A. dip them in a sterilizing solution
    B. wash them with a strong detergent
    C. boil them in the sterilizer
    D. steam them under pressure

2. Sterilization by use of chemicals rather than by boiling water is indicated when the instrument   2.____

    A. is made of soft rubber
    B. has a sharp cutting edge
    C. has pus or blood on it
    D. was used more than 24 hours before sterilization

3. When dusting the furniture in the clinic, it is advisable to use a silicone-treated dustcloth CHIEFLY because the treated cloth will   3.____

    A. collect the dust more efficiently
    B. disinfect as well as dust the furniture
    C. not remove the wax from the furniture
    D. make it unnecessary to polish the furniture in the future

4. Assume that the clinic in which you work has issued instructions that all supplies containing poison are to have blue labels with the word *poison* clearly marked on the label, and that these supplies are to be kept in a storage cabinet separate from other supplies. You notice that a bottle with no label is on a shelf in the *poison* storage cabinet.
   Of the following, the BEST action for you to take is to   4.____

    A. place the unlabeled bottle in the back of the regular storage cabinet
    B. put a blue label on the bottle and write *poison* on the label
    C. ask another public health employee to help you decide if the bottle contains poison
    D. pour the contents of the bottle into the slop sink and destroy the bottle

5. Assume that you have been assigned to care for the supply room, and have been instructed to use the items which have been in stock longest before using the newer stock. Of the following, the MOST practical and time-saving way to do this is to   5.____

    A. keep a record file of all supplies received and used
    B. write the dates when the supplies were received and used on the labels or containers
    C. place new supplies behind supplies of the same items already in stock
    D. keep the fastest moving stock in the most convenient places

57

6. The public health employee should know that clinic supplies should be reordered
   A. as soon as the last container of the item in the supply closet is used up
   B. in the same amount on the first working day of each month
   C. whenever a let-up in clinic work makes time available
   D. when the records show that the stock may possibly be depleted within a month

7. The CHIEF reason for storing x-ray film in lead containers is that lead containers protect the film from
   A. moisture in the atmosphere
   B. exposure to stray x-rays
   C. dust and other particles
   D. extreme changes in temperature

8. You have been instructed to keep all narcotics locked in a separate cabinet when storing supplies.
   The one of the following which should be kept locked in this cabinet is a preparation containing
   A. cortisone   B. codeine   C. caffeine   D. quinine

9. Of the following medical supplies, the one which should be refrigerated is
   A. vaseline jelly   B. paregoric
   C. aureomycin   D. aspirin tablets

10. The one of the following which is NOT an antiseptic or disinfectant is
    A. distilled water   B. alcohol
    C. lysol   D. hydrogen peroxide

11. The one of the following which is an anesthetic is
    A. novocaine   B. phenobarbital
    C. benzedrine   D. witch hazel

12. The wide use of antibiotics has presented a number of problems. Some patients become allergic to the drugs so that they cannot be used when they are needed. In other cases, after prolonged treatment with antibiotics, certain organisms no longer respond to them at all. This is one of the reasons for the constant search for more potent drugs.
    On the basis of this paragraph, the one of the following statements which is MOST NEARLY correct is that
    A. antibiotics have been used successfully for certain allergies
    B. antibiotics should never be used for prolonged treatment
    C. because they have developed an allergy to the drug, antibiotics cannot be used when needed for certain patients
    D. one of the reasons for the constant search for new antibiotics is that so many diseases have been successfully treated with these drugs

3 (#2)

13. The over-use of antibiotics today represents a growing danger, according to many medical authorities. Patients everywhere, stimulated by reports of new wonder drugs, continue to ask their doctors for a shot to relieve a cold, grippe, or any of the other virus infections that occur during the course of a bad winter. But, for the common cold and many other virus infections, antibiotics have no effect.
On the basis of this paragraph, the one of the following statements which is MOST NEARLY correct is that

    A. the use of antibiotics is becoming a health hazard
    B. antibiotics are of no value in the treatment of many virus infections
    C. patients should ask their doctors for a shot of one of the new wonder drugs to relieve the symptoms of grippe
    D. the treatment of colds and other virus infections by antibiotics will lessen their severity

13.____

14. Statistics tell us that heart disease kills more people than any other illness, and the death rate still continues to rise. People over 30 have a fifty-fifty chance of escaping, for heart disease is chiefly an illness of people in late middle age and advanced years. Because there are more people in this age group living today than there were some years ago, heart disease is able to find more victims.
On the basis of this paragraph, the one of the following statements which is MOST NEARLY correct is that

    A. half of the people over 30 years of age have heart disease today
    B. more people die of heart disease than of all other diseases combined
    C. older people are the chief victims of heart disease
    D. the rising birth rate has increased the possibility that the average person will die of heart disease

14.____

15. There is evidence that some individuals, given three doses of polio vaccine, have not developed enough immunity to protect themselves against paralytic polio. It is thought that immunity will be increased by a fourth injection given no sooner than one year after the third injection and many health agencies have been giving a fourth injection to their patients.
On the basis of this paragraph, the one of the following statements which is MOST NEARLY correct is that

    A. three doses of polio vaccine will not give any protection from paralytic polio
    B. a fourth injection of polio vaccine guarantees immunity to polio
    C. the fourth injection of polio vaccine should be given as soon as possible after the third injection
    D. the fourth injection of polio vaccine should be given at least a year after the third injection

15.____

Questions 16-22.

DIRECTIONS: Questions 16 through 22 are to be answered on the basis of the following table.

REPORT ON PATIENTS ATTENDING SELECTED HEALTH CLINICS January to December (This Year)					
CLINICS	A	B	C	D	E
Child Health	62,400	70,200	81,900	83,400	22,300
Chest	53,300	52,000	64,800	47,600	4,500
Social Hygiene	24,500	21,900	18,400	13,500	4,100
Eye	10,600	12,600	13,300	13,800	4,200
Cardiac	1,400	1,600	1,700	1,300	400
Prenatal	1,300	1,800	1,700	1,800	500

16. On the basis of the above chart, the group with the LARGEST number of patients attending the eye clinics was

    A. B   B. C   C. A   D. D

17. If the population of the area located around group E was 210,000, the percentage of this population who attended the eye clinic was MOST NEARLY

    A. .02%   B. 2%   C. 5%   D. 21%

18. If the clinics were open 250 days, the average daily attendance at the social hygiene clinics in group C was MOST NEARLY

    A. 74   B. 88   C. 259   D. 736

19. The percentage of all patients attending group E clinics who attended the chest clinics was MOST NEARLY

    A. 5%   B. 8%   C. 13%   D. 25%

20. If 25% of the patients attending prenatal clinics in group B also attended the cardiac clinics, the number of prenatal clinic patients in group B who did NOT attend the cardiac clinics was MOST NEARLY

    A. 400   B. 450   C. 1200   D. 1350

21. If the number of persons who attended all clinics in group A last year was 20% less than this year, the number who attended the group A clinics last year was MOST NEARLY

    A. 32,700   B. 130,800   C. 163,500   D. 196,200

22. Assume that at the end of the year it was found that half of the people who attended the group B chest clinics had been found to be free of disease, 1/3 were discharged as needing no further care, and the rest were instructed to return to the clinic for further treatment.
    The number of persons who were told to return for further treatment was MOST NEARLY

    A. 7,000   B. 14,000   C. 21,000   D. 35,000

Questions 23-34.

5 (#2)

DIRECTIONS: Each of Questions 23 through 34 consists of a word, in capitals, followed by four suggested meanings of the word. For each question, indicate in the space at the right the letter preceding the word which means MOST NEARLY the same as the word in capitals.

23. PUNCTUAL 23.____
    A. usual   B. hollow
    C. infrequent   D. on time

24. BENEFICIAL 24.____
    A. popular   B. forceful   C. helpful   D. necessary

25. TEMPORARY 25.____
    A. permanently   B. for a limited time
    C. at the same time D. frequently

26. INQUIRE 26.____
    A. order   B. agree   C. ask   D. discharge

27. SUFFICIENT 27.____
    A. enough   B. inadequate
    C. thorough   D. capable

28. AMBULATORY 28.____
    A. bedridden   B. lefthanded
    C. walking   D. laboratory

29. DILATE 29.____
    A. enlarge   B. contract   C. revise   D. restrict

30. NUTRITIOUS 30.____
    A. protective   B. healthful
    C. fattening   D. nourishing

31. CONGENITAL 31.____
    A. with pleasure   B. defective
    C. likeable   D. existing from birth

32. ISOLATION 32.____
    A. sanitation   B. quarantine
    C. rudeness   D. exposure

33. SPASM 33.____
    A. splash   B. twitch   C. space   D. blow

34. HEMORRHAGE 34.____
    A. bleeding   B. ulcer
    C. hereditary disease D. lack of blood

Questions 35-40.

DIRECTIONS: Questions 35 through 40 are to be answered on the basis of the usual rules for alphabetical filing. For each question, indicate in the space at the right the letter preceding the name which should be filed THIRD in alphabetical order.

35. A. Hesselberg, Norman J. B. Hesselman, Nathan B. 35.___
    C. Hazel, Robert S.   D. Heintz, August J.

36. A. Oshins, Jerome   B. Ohsie, Marjorie   36.___
    C. O'Shaugn, F.J.   D. O'Shea, Frances

37. A. Petrie, Joshua A.   B. Pendleton, Oscar   37.___
    C. Pertweee, Joshua   D. Perkins, Warren G.

38. A. Morganstern, Alfred   B. Morganstern, Albert   38.___
    C. Monroe, Mildred   D. Modesti, Ernest

39. A. More, Stewart   B. Moorhead, Jay   39.___
    C. Moore, Benjamin   D. Moffat, Edith

40. A. Ramirez, Paul   B. Revere, Pauline   40.___
    C. Ramos, Felix   D. Ramazotti, Angelo

Questions 41-50.

DIRECTIONS: Questions 41 through 50 are to be answered on the basis of the usual rules of filing. Column I lists the names of 10 clinic patients. Column II lists the headings of file drawers into which you are to place the records of these patients. For each question, indicate in the space at the right the letter preceding the heading of the file drawer in which the record should be filed.

COLUMN I   COLUMN II

41. Charles Coughlin   A. Cab-Cep   41.___

42. Mary Carstairs   B. Ceq-Cho   42.___

43. Joseph Collin   C. Chr-Coj   43.___

44. Thomas Chelsey   D. Cok-Czy   44.___

45. Cedric Chalmers   45.___

46. Mae Clarke   46.___

47. Dora Copperhead   47.___

48. Arnold Cohn   48.___

49. Charlotte Crumboldt   49.___

50. Frances Celine   50.___

KEY (CORRECT ANSWERS)

1. D	11. A	21. B	31. D	41. D
2. B	12. C	22. A	32. B	42. A
3. A	13. B	23. D	33. B	43. D
4. D	14. C	24. C	34. A	44. B
5. C	15. D	25. B	35. A	45. B
6. D	16. D	26. C	36. D	46. C
7. B	17. B	27. A	37. C	47. D
8. B	18. A	28. C	38. B	48. C
9. C	19. C	29. A	39. B	49. D
10. A	20. D	30. D	40. C	50. A

EXAMINATION SECTION
TEST 1

DIRECTIONS: Each question or incomplete statement is followed by several suggested answers or completions. Select the one that BEST answers the question or completes the statement. *PRINT THE LETTER OF THE CORRECT ANSWER IN THE SPACE AT THE RIGHT.*

1. Multiphasic screening, now adopted by many health departments, is BEST defined as a   1.____

    A. new method of testing vision
    B. case finding procedure combining tests for several diseases
    C. combined vision and hearing test
    D. new method of cancer detection

2. Of the following statements that a nurse might make to a patient ill with cancer who says, *I don't think I'll ever get better. When the pain comes, I'm afraid I'll die before anyone gets here,* the one which would be MOST appropriate is: 2.____

    A. I wouldn't worry about that. People do not die because of pain.
    B. Of course you'll get better. You look much better than you did the last time I was here.
    C. You should try to have someone here with you and not be alone. Then you won't be afraid.
    D. I think I understand how you feel, but why do you think you won't get better?

3. In an epidemiological study of a disease, the one of the following steps which would usually NOT be included is   3.____

    A. collecting and compiling data on the incidence, prevalence, and trends of the disease
    B. reviewing the *natural history* of the disease
    C. making a sociological study of the community in which the disease is prevalent
    D. defining gaps in knowledge and developing hypotheses on which to base further investigation

4. Adequate lighting in the school is an important part of the sight conservation program. The school nurse familiar with standards for classroom lighting should know that the RECOMMENDED illumination on each desk for ordinary classroom work is _____ candles.   4.____

    A. 20-foot   B. 35-foot   C. 50-foot   D. 75-foot

5. The relation of fluorine to dental health has been the subject of extensive study for many years.
Of the following statements concerning the relation of fluorine to dental caries, the one which is CORRECT is that   5.____

    A. mass medication by fluorine is now accepted as the best means of treating and curing dental caries
    B. fluoridation of water supplies, though effective, is too expensive for wide usage
    C. fluoridation is effective only in children born in areas in which fluoridation exists
    D. fluoridation prevents dental caries but does not treat or cure it

6. There are measures which are effective in the prevention of diabetes in those with an hereditary disposition.
   Of the following, the one which has the GREATEST value as a preventive measure is

   A. preventing acute infection
   B. preventing obesity
   C. avoidance of emotional stress
   D. avoidance of marriage with a known diabetic

7. The basis of a program of *natural childbirth* is to

   A. prevent or dispel fear through education in the physiology of pregnancy
   B. reduce premature births and the complications of pregnancy
   C. reduce the maternal and neonatal mortality rates
   D. prepare the mother's body for the muscular activity of delivery

8. The one of the following statements which is CORRECT concerning retrolental fibroplasia is that it is a

   A. blood dyscrasia
   B. condition occurring in Rh negative infants whose mothers are Rh positive
   C. condition causing blindness in premature infants
   D. complication of congenital syphilis

9. Of the following factors, the one which is MOST important in maintaining optimum health in the older age group is

   A. regular medical supervision for early recognition and treatment of minor symptoms
   B. economic independence which gives a feeling of security
   C. avoidance of all emotional tensions
   D. adjustment of the environment to prevent physical and mental strain

10. The MOST outstanding result of antibiotic therapy in the treatment of syphilis has been to

    A. reduce the toxic effect of treatment
    B. shorten the treatment period
    C. prevent a relapse
    D. prevent late complications

11. To achieve the most effective and economical case finding for tuberculosis, mass examinations should be conducted PRIMARILY for

    A. infants under one year
    B. industrial workers
    C. elementary school students
    D. pre-school age group

12. Though tuberculosis occurs in all age groups, there is a certain period of life when individuals have the greatest resistance to the infection.
    That period is

    A. under one year of age
    B. between 3 years and puberty
    C. between 15 and 35 years of age
    D. between 25 and 40 years of age

13. Drug therapy for tuberculosis has proven to be an important tool in the control of the disease in its active stage.
    Of the following, the one which has had the MOST satisfactory results to date in that fewer patients develop resistance to the drug and the incidence of drug toxicity is reduced is

    A. para-amino-salicylic acid (P.A.S.) in combination with streptomycin
    B. dihydro-streptomycin
    C. streptomycin in combination with promine
    D. penicillin

    13.____

14. Studies have indicated that the use of streptomycin in the treatment of tuberculosis has GREATEST value in

    A. recently developed pneumonic or exudative lesions
    B. long standing infections which have been resistant to other therapies
    C. military T.B.
    D. meningeal T.B.

    14.____

15. The PARTICULAR effectiveness of chemotherapeutic agents in the treatment of pulmonary tuberculosis is that they

    A. are important adjuncts to surgery
    B. inhibit the growth of the bacillus
    C. heal lesions rapidly
    D. render the patient non-infectious

    15.____

KEY (CORRECT ANSWERS)

1. B
2. D
3. C
4. A
5. D

6. B
7. A
8. C
9. A
10. B

11. B
12. B
13. A
14. A
15. B

TEST 2

DIRECTIONS: Each question or incomplete statement is followed by several suggested answers or completions. Select the one that BEST answers the question or completes the statement. *PRINT THE LETTER OF THE CORRECT ANSWER IN THE SPACE AT THE RIGHT.*

1. The CHIEF shortcoming of chemotherapeutic agents in the treatment of pulmonary tuberculosis is

    A. their prohibitive cost in any long-term treatment
    B. the toxic effects which follow their use
    C. that their use is limited to early cases
    D. the development of bacterial resistance by the host

2. Though precise knowledge concerning the optimum duration of chemotherapy in treating pulmonary tuberculosis is lacking, the present APPROVED practice is

    A. continued uninterrupted treatment until the sputum is negative
    B. short courses of treatment with rest periods in between
    C. continued treatment for a minimum of 12 months
    D. continued treatment for one year after a negative sputum and cultures are obtained

3. A community program for the control of tuberculosis must include school children and school personnel if it is to be a success.
   Of the following statements, the one which BEST represents expert opinion on the use of B.C.G. vaccine in the school program for tuberculosis control is that

    A. through immunization of all school children it serves as an important control measure
    B. its chief value is that it is an inexpensive and rapid method of case finding
    C. it would nullify the subsequent use of the tuberculin test which is the best case finding method for schools
    D. it is a valuable diagnostic method which would reduce the evidence of contact with active cases

4. Nutritional deficiencies are a common problem in geriatrics.
   The dietary adjustment usually necessary to maintain PROPER nutrition for the average person in the older age group is

    A. increased proteins and vitamins
    B. elimination of fats
    C. increased carbohydrates
    D. elimination of roughage

5. The death rate from cancer can be reduced by early diagnosis and treatment. It is important, therefore, for the nurse to assist in case finding.
   She should know that, of the following sites, the one which the GREATEST incidence of cancer in women occurs is the

    A. mouth   B. skin   C. breast   D. rectum

6. Many cancers appear to develop when pre-existing abnormal conditions and changes in the tissue are present.
   Of the following, the one which is at present considered PRECANCEROUS is

   A. fibroid tumor
   B. chronic cervicitis
   C. fat tissue tumor
   D. sebaceous cyst

7. The diagnosis of cancer by examination of isolated cells in body secretions is known as

   A. biopsy
   B. aspiration technique
   C. histological diagnosis
   D. Papanicolaou smear

8. Of the following statements concerning our present knowledge of the etiology of human cancer, the one which is TRUE is that

   A. there is definite evidence that some cancers are caused by a virus
   B. some types of cancer are definitely contagious
   C. there is a strong possibility that cancer is transmitted from mother to baby in utero
   D. so many factors are involved that the discovery of a single cause is unlikely

9. The National Venereal Disease Control Program carried on by the Public Health Service of the U.S. Government is concerned PRIMARILY with

   A. promoting medical programs to provide early effective treatment of infected individuals
   B. a national program of education in the prevention of venereal diseases
   C. distribution of free drugs to physicians for the treatment of venereal disease
   D. providing funds for the education of physicians and nurses in the treatment and care of venereal disease

10. Of the following, the one which is of GREATEST importance in the prevention of poliomyelitis is to

    A. build up resistance with proper diet
    B. keep away from crowds during periods when the disease is prevalent
    C. immunize with gamma globulin
    D. adopt general public health measures for the protection of food and water

11. Of the following statements concerning the present status of chemotherapy in the treatment of cancer, the one which is TRUE is:

    A. Results to date indicate it may soon surpass radiation and surgery as an effective cure
    B. It has not proven effective except in cases where early diagnosis was made
    C. It must be used in conjunction with radiation or surgery
    D. It inhibits the growth of certain types of cancer and prolongs life but is not effective as a cure

12. The W.H.O. Regional Organization for Europe has set up a long-term plan for European health needs.
    Of the following activities, the one which is NOT planned as a major activity is

A. coordinating health policies in European countries
B. promoting improved service through demonstration of an ideal health program in one country
C. promoting professional and technical education for health workers in the member countries
D. providing for exchange of services among member nations

13. A health problem becomes the concern of public health authorities when the incidence is great and the mortality rate high.
In terms of this statement, of the following problems, the one which should be a PRIMARY concern is

   A. venereal diseases in young adults
   B. tuberculosis
   C. tropical diseases among ex-servicemen and their families
   D. degenerative diseases of middle and later life

14. Of the following, the one which is now considered to be the MOST common mode of transmission of poliomyelitis is

   A. infected insects
   B. contaminated water
   C. personal contact
   D. infected food

15. The incubation period for infantile paralysis is

   A. usually 7 to 14 days, but may vary from 3 to 35 days
   B. not known
   C. one week
   D. usually 48 hours, but may vary from 1 to 7 days

KEY (CORRECT ANSWERS)

1. D
2. C
3. C
4. A
5. C
6. B
7. D
8. D
9. A
10. B
11. D
12. B
13. D
14. C
15. A

EXAMINATION SECTION
TEST 1

DIRECTIONS: Each question or incomplete statement is followed by several suggested answers or completions. Select the one that BEST answers the question or completes the statement. *PRINT THE LETTER OF THE CORRECT ANSWER IN THE SPACE AT THE RIGHT.*

1. Normally, upon exposure to air, blood clots form within _____ minutes.   1.____

   A. 30 seconds to two
   B. three to ten
   C. ten to fifteen
   D. fifteen to thirty

2. The red blood cells of the body are produced in the   2.____

   A. spongy area of the long bones, in the ribs, and in the vertebrae
   B. ends of the long bones and the spleen
   C. liver and the flat bones
   D. pancreas and the liver

3. All of the following statements are correct EXCEPT: 3.____

   A. The figures used for the recording of blood pressure represent in millimeters the height of a column of mercury in the sphygmomanometer.
   B. In high blood pressure cases, progressive damage to the blood vessels takes place, whereas hypertension is limited to harder than normal work by the heart to pump the same amount of blood around to the tissues.
   C. In the recording of blood pressure, the larger figure represents the maximum pressure in the arteries with each heart beat.
   D. The smaller figure in the recording of an individual's blood pressure registers the minimum pressure between heart beats.

4. The physician can actually see the arteries and veins at work when he   4.____

   A. measures the pressure of the walls of the blood vessels
   B. uses the ophthalmoscope in examining the eyes
   C. applies a fluoroscope in examining a patient
   D. uses the electrocardiograph

5. The blood-clotting process in the body is started by the breaking up of   5.____

   A. plasma
   B. platelets
   C. white blood cells
   D. red blood cells

6. The condition that impairs the elasticity and function of the blood vessel walls and reduces the volume of blood that may pass through the afflicted arteries is   6.____

   A. hypertension
   B. vascular occlusion
   C. high blood pressure
   D. hardening of the arteries

7. All of the following statements are correct EXCEPT: 7.____

   A. There is more limited mobility of the big toe of the foot compared to that of the thumb on the hand.

B. The foot bones are held together in such a way as to form springy lengthwise and crosswise arches.
C. The much greater solidity of the big toe as compared to the fingers on the hand help the foot to support body weight.
D. The phalanges of the foot are relatively more important than those of the hand and have a greater role in the functioning of the foot than those in the hand.

8. The inside of the shaft of a long bone is filled with

   A. yellow marrow
   B. compact bony cells
   C. red blood cells
   D. gelatinous tissue

9. Children's bones do not break so easily as those of older persons because their bones

   A. are less flexible
   B. do not carry so heavy a weight
   C. contain more cartilage
   D. receive better nutritional foods

10. All of the following associations are correct EXCEPT:

    A. Intracutaneous - within the layers of the skin
    B. Hypodermic - beneath the skin
    C. Subcutaneous - sweat glands over the entire skin surface
    D. Diaphoresis - perceptible perspiration

11. The PRIMARY purpose of melanin is to

    A. provide variation in the toughness of the skin
    B. prevent the more dangerous rays of the sun from damaging tissues
    C. convert surface skin on certain parts of the body into horny material
    D. dilate the blood vessels in the skin

12. Of the following, the SAFEST treatment for corns on toes is to

    A. apply a medicated moleskin plaster to the area
    B. wear well-fitted shoes
    C. cut off the mass of dead skin cells on the surface of the corn
    D. apply a corn remover

13. Of the following statements, the CORRECT one is:

    A. Suntan preparations enable an individual to stay in the sun longer with less risk of burning than without their use.
    B. Suntan lotions increase the speed of one's natural tanning mechanism.
    C. Suntan preparations shut out burning ultraviolet rays.
    D. The application of suntan preparations is more effective when used during exposure to direct mid-day hours of sun rather than used on hazy, lightly overcast days.

14. To soften water,

    A. calcium in a fluid state is added to the water supply
    B. fluorides in small amounts are added to the water supply
    C. sodium is substituted for the calcium and magnesium in the water
    D. sodium is taken from the water supply by the addition of chlorine

15. All of the following are important in tooth development EXCEPT vitamin   15.____

    A. A	B. C	C. B	D. D

16. Of the following, the gland MOST closely related to muscular efficiency is the   16.____

    A. adrenal	B. gonads	C. pituitary	D. thyroid

17. The INCORRECT association of gland and location is: 17.____

    A. Pineal - brain cavity
    B. Parotid - below and in front of the ear
    C. Submaxillary - below each lower jaw
    D. Thymus - at the larynx

18. A urine analysis does NOT test for the   18.____

    A. possibility of diabetes
    B. presence of albumin
    C. evidence of bladder or kidney inflammation
    D. growth of polyps in the urinary tract

19. All of the following are basic taste sensations EXCEPT _____ sensations.   19.____

    A. hot and cold	B. sweet
    C. bitter	D. sour

20. The accumulation of an oxygen debt by a normally healthy individual engaged in sport activity is related MOST directly to   20.____

    A. lack of endurance
    B. limited residual air
    C. strenuous exercise
    D. failure of the hemoglobin to combine with oxygen

21. The CHIEF cause of heart disease in persons under 40 years of age is   21.____

    A. heredity	B. rheumatic fever
    C. obesity	D. elevated blood pressure

22. Binocular vision is MOST important in   22.____

    A. forming impressions of depth
    B. providing a clear image of item on which eyes are focused
    C. reducing strain in each of the eyes
    D. intensifying receipt of light rays on the retina

23. The INCORRECT association is: 23.____

    A. Cornea - transparent part of the outer layer of the eye
    B. Lens - part of the eye where light first enters to be focused on the retina
    C. Iris - muscle which controls the size of the pupil
    D. Sclera - hard protective outer layer of the eye

24. Of the following, the CORRECT statement is: 24.____

    A. Wearing eyeglasses will always make a person's eyes stronger.

B. If a person is able to see clearly, he can be sure he doesn't need glasses.
C. Glancing occasionally at some distant object when doing close work with the eyes helps prevent eye strain.
D. Wearing sunglasses gives the eyes complete protection from the sun.

25. All of the following are correct reasons as to why it is necessary to maintain good posture when reading a book EXCEPT:

    A. Reading with the head bent forward strains the neck muscles
    B. Viewing print at a sharp angle strains the eye muscles in their effort to focus
    C. Studying a page in a book while lying down distorts the image on the page
    D. Interpreting the printed page while sitting in a slouched position results in eye inflammation

26. In order to avoid eye fatigue during the viewing of a television program, the lighting arrangement in the room should provide light that

    A. is reflected on the screen
    B. brings about subdued general illumination of the room
    C. provides sharp contrast between the television screen and the surrounding area
    D. is located in the line of vision toward the screen

27. The SAFEST method of acquiring a suntan is the one in which

    A. a preparation is applied to provide a protective covering during the exposure time
    B. gradual exposure allows the skin to build natural resistance by increased pigmentation and thickening for an even tanning
    C. exposure of the skin is started with reflected rays from water rather than from morning rays of direct sunlight
    D. skin is exposed to noon-day rays

28. No amount of vitamin D will serve to promote normal bone development unless the diet includes, in adequate quantities,

    A. calcium and phosphorus   B. sodium and sulfur
    C. iron and magnesium   D. potassium and carbon

29. All of the following associations concerning milk are correct EXCEPT:

    A. Pasteurization - destruction of the common pathogens found in milk
    B. Homogenization - process of emulsifying milk
    C. Irradiation - sterilization of raw milk
    D. Centrifugalization - separation of cream from the milk

30. It is INCORRECT to state that cholesterol

    A. metabolism is related to atherosclerosis
    B. is a normal and essential constituent of human tissue
    C. levels in the blood are related to intake of animal fats
    D. levels in the blood are lowered by intake of saturated fats

31. Of the following, the one that is NOT an after-effect of rickets is

    A. bow-legs   B. chicken breast
    C. knock-knees   D. clubfoot

32. All of the following concerning amino acids are correct EXCEPT:

    A. All amino acids contain carbon, hydrogen, oxygen, and nitrogen
    B. Excess amino acids are stored in the involuntary musculature of the body
    C. Proteins are made up of amino acids
    D. Amino acids play an important role in maintaining both natural and acquired resistance to infection

33. Of the following, the CORRECT statement is:

    A. All people with rosy complexions are healthy
    B. Any food that does not smell or taste spoiled is safe to eat
    C. All children with heart murmurs will surely have heart trouble later on in life
    D. Most persons who look thin and underweight are not necessarily in poor health

34. In your health guidance period, you have a pupil with a long, thin trunk. Classifying by somatotypes, you would list this pupil as a(n)

    A. mesomorph   B. endomorph   C. holomorph   D. ectomorph

35. All of the following associations are correct EXCEPT:

    A. Muscle cramp - sustained involuntary contractions
    B. Muscle twitch - minor irregular spasm
    C. Muscle spasticity - sustained tension
    D. Muscle hypertrophy - decreased size due to loss of elasticity

36. All of the following statements are correct EXCEPT: The

    A. mitral valve is between the left auricle and the left ventricle
    B. tricuspid valve is between the right auricle and the right ventricle
    C. aortic-semilunar valve is between the aorta and the right auricle
    D. pulmonary semilunar valve is between the right ventricle and the pulmonary artery

37. Urea is made in the

    A. kidneys   B. liver
    C. ureter   D. urinary bladder

38. Definite sensory centers in the brain have been found for all of the following EXCEPT

    A. hearing   B. pain   C. vision   D. equilibrium

39. Saliva is associated with all of the following glands EXCEPT the

    A. submaxillary   B. parotid
    C. fundic   D. sublingual

40. Plasma is more advantageous than whole blood in an emergency because it

    A. contains more white corpuscles
    B. does not have to be typed
    C. contains more red corpuscles
    D. contains more platelets

41. The last year was characterized by a decrease in all of the following EXCEPT

    A. poliomyelitis cases
    B. tuberculosis deaths
    C. infant and maternal deaths from childbirth
    D. heart disease and blood vessel disturbances

42. All of the following associations are correct EXCEPT:

    A. Paul Burkholder - chloromycetin
    B. Philip Hench - cortisone
    C. Selman Waksman - streptomycin
    D. Benjamin Duggar - insulin

43. Tobacco has the effect of temporarily decreasing the appetite because it causes an increased concentration of blood

    A. sugar   B. protein   C. salts   D. starches

44. The present state of research in the relationship between the incidence of lung cancer and smoking indicates the presence of a definite relationship between lung cancer and

    A. cigarette smoking
    B. pipe smoking
    C. cigar smoking
    D. all of the above

45. If a pupil is overweight only because of food intake, the teacher can help guide him by all of the following admonitions EXCEPT:

    A. *Gradually change your eating habits*
    B. *Eliminate your breakfast*
    C. *Be content to reduce slowly*
    D. *Practice self-control*

46. All of the following are enzymes of pancreatic juice EXCEPT

    A. amylopsin   B. ptyalin   C. steapsin   D. trypsin

47. A sprain in any part of the body PRIMARILY involves the _____ tissue.

    A. ligament   B. nerve   C. skin   D. muscle

48. A victim with a fractured neck should ALWAYS be transported lying on

    A. the stomach, face downward
    B. a stretcher
    C. his back, face upward
    D. a blanket

49. All of the following statements are correct EXCEPT

    A. In a fracture, crepitus is usually present, but in a dislocation there is no crepitus.
    B. In a fracture, deformity may vary in extent while in a dislocation, the deformity is usually marked.

C. In a dislocation, deformity recurs after the part is placed in its normal position, while in a fracture there is no deformity after the bone is placed in normal position.
D. In a dislocation, the head of the bone rotates with the rest of the bone, whereas in a fracture the bone moves as two bones or as a bone with a loose end.

50. All of the following are complete fractures EXCEPT a(n) _____ fracture. 50.____

    A. impacted   B. greenstick   C. Colles'   D. Pott's

KEY (CORRECT ANSWERS)

1. B	11. B	21. B	31. D	41. D
2. A	12. B	22. A	32. B	42. D
3. B	13. A	23. B	33. D	43. A
4. B	14. C	24. C	34. D	44. A
5. B	15. C	25. D	35. D	45. B
6. D	16. A	26. B	36. C	46. B
7. D	17. D	27. B	37. B	47. A
8. A	18. D	28. A	38. B	48. C
9. C	19. A	29. C	39. C	49. C
10. C	20. C	30. D	40. B	50. B

TEST 2

DIRECTIONS: Each question or incomplete statement is followed by several suggested answers or completions. Select the one that BEST answers the question or completes the statement. *PRINT THE LETTER OF THE CORRECT ANSWER IN THE SPACE AT THE RIGHT.*

1. The stimulant theobromine is found in all of the following EXCEPT   1.___

    A. cocoa   B. chocolate   C. tea   D. coffee

2. Recent research indicates that the appetite center or food intake control is located in the   2.___

    A. pancreatic gland
    B. hypothalamus located at the base of the brain
    C. nerve centers that are directly controlled by the big muscles
    D. duodenum

3. In general, all of the following act to reduce the vitamin content in any food EXCEPT   3.___

    A. storage at room temperature for long periods
    B. freezing
    C. excessive heat
    D. prolonged cooking

4. All of the following are vitamins EXCEPT   4.___

    A. thiamine   B. niacin   C. heparin   D. biotin

5. All of the following associations are correct EXCEPT: 5.___

    A. Antidermatitis - vitamin B_6
    B. Antihemorrhagic - vitamin K
    C. Antineuritic - vitamin B_1
    D. Antisterility - vitamin G

6. All of the following associations are correct EXCEPT: 6.___

    A. Sodium and potassium - normal beating of heart
    B. Iron and copper - making of hemoglobin
    C. Calcium and phosphorus - formation of bone
    D. Chlorine and sulphur - oxidative processes

7. Dry skim milk   7.___

    A. has the same butterfat content as homogenized milk
    B. contains considerably more fat and vitamin A than whole milk
    C. has butterfat removed
    D. loses a good deal of its nutritional value when stored for several months

8. A pupil should be referred for the pitch tone test if the FINAL score in the first audiometer test screening shows a hearing loss of

   A. 1 to 5 decibels in both ears
   B. 6 to 9 decibels in one ear
   C. 12 or more decibels in one or both ears
   D. 9 decibels in both ears

9. MOST cases of deafness are caused by troubles in the

   A. outer ear
   B. inner ear
   C. eustachian tube
   D. middle ear

10. After a group of pupils has had the audiometer test and before another group of pupils uses the ear phones, it is advisable for the teacher to

    A. cleanse the ear phones with alcohol and cotton
    B. dip the ear phones in a solution of peroxide and water
    C. continue the testing without touching the ear phones
    D. tell the next group of pupils to rub the ear phones with a handkerchief or piece of tissue

11. In MOST large cities, sewage is purified by

    A. aeration
    B. chemical action
    C. exposure to sunlight
    D. isolation

12. The use of hard water for bathing is less satisfactory than the use of soft water because of all of the following reasons EXCEPT:

    A. Hard water contains more calcium and magnesium than soft water
    B. Hydrolysis is slower in hard water than in soft water
    C. The use of detergents made necessary by bathing in hard water produces a drying effect on the skin
    D. The additional use of soap and the more vigorous rubbing required by the use of hard water may irritate the skin

13. Research on the fluoridation of public water supplies at the recommended concentration indicates that

    A. there is a significant difference in the general death rate between areas where fluoride is present and those where it is absent
    B. the amount of fluoride useful for the prevention of tooth decay is well below the toxic level
    C. the continued consumption of water treated with fluoride is harmful to adults suffering from chronic illnesses
    D. the fluoridation of water has caused a comparatively high incidence of disfiguring mottled tooth enamel

14. The poisonous character of carbon monoxide is due to its tendency to unite chemically with

    A. synovial fluid
    B. cerebro-spinal fluid
    C. hemoglobin
    D. gastric juice

15. With regard to a tourniquet, the one CORRECT first aid procedure, according to the American Red Cross, is

    A. loosening it after 20 minutes
    B. having it released only by a physician
    C. placing it on the wound
    D. having it applied only by a physician or nurse

16. Of the following procedures for the periodic check-up of pupils' height and weight by the health guidance teacher, the MOST desirable is the one in which the teacher

    A. judges the pupil's height and weight and records his (her) judgment as satisfactory or unsatisfactory on the pupil's health envelope
    B. asks the pupil whether he has increased in height and lost or gained any weight and records the answers on the pupil's health envelope
    C. measures but does not record the pupil's height and weight on the pupil's record since variations in these items indicate that height-weight charts are obsolete
    D. measures the pupil's height and weight and records the findings as a means of evaluating the cumulative record of growth of the pupil

17. In cases of lordosis, there is a marked tendency to assume a position of round shoulders because in such cases,

    A. the body compensates for the backward shifting of the body weight
    B. too much weight is thrown on the forward edges of the lumbar vertebrae
    C. the erector spinal muscles in the thoracic region are shortened
    D. the pelvis tilts backward

18. All of the following associations of conditions and causes are correct EXCEPT:

    A. Carbuncle - infection of a sebaceous gland
    B. Wart - excessive growth of papillae of the skin
    C. Mole - overdevelopment of pigment cells under the epidermis
    D. Boil - infection, usually at the site of a hair follicle

19. All of the following associations are correct EXCEPT:

    A. Macula - point of clearest vision at the center of the retina
    B. Organ of corti - sense of hearing
    C. Tympanic membrane - sound vibrations
    D. Mastoid cells - body balance

20. All of the following associations are correct EXCEPT:

    A. Peristalsis - wavelike contractions that pass along a tube
    B. Catalysis - breaking down of body cells
    C. Catharsis - purgation
    D. Metastasis - transfer of disease from a primary focus to a distant one

21. A lesion in the cerebellum may cause

    A. aphasia   B. ataxia   C. atavism   D. asthenia

22. All of the following associations concerning inflammation are correct EXCEPT: 22.____

    A. Heat - calor
    B. Redness - rubor
    C. Pain - dolor
    D. Swelling - aden

23. When the term *febrile* is associated with a physical condition, it means that the condition is characterized by 23.____

    A. fibroids
    B. weakness of an organ
    C. fever
    D. decreased respiration

24. All of the following associations are correct EXCEPT: 24.____

    A. Hepatic - pertaining to the liver
    B. Herpetic - pertaining to hair
    C. Hemiplegic - pertaining to paralysis of one side of the body
    D. Hematic - pertaining to the blood

25. All of the following are important components of the visual act proper EXCEPT 25.____

    A. accommodation
    B. interpretation
    C. convergence
    D. fusion

26. Of the following, the LEAST desirable practice in viewing television is to 26.____

    A. have the room dark
    B. view the screen from directly in front
    C. have moderate indirect lighting of the room
    D. frequently shift the eyes away from the screen

27. Of the following, the INCORRECT association is: 27.____

    A. Sclera - white of the eye
    B. Cornea - window of the eye
    C. Lens - pupil of the eye
    D. Iris - shutter of the eye

28. If the length of the anteroposterior diameter of the eye is too great, the resulting condition is 28.____

    A. farsightedness
    B. nearsightedness
    C. astigmatism
    D. trachoma

29. When the health guidance teacher tests pupils' vision by means of the Snellen chart, he(she) is testing the pupils' 29.____

    A. near acuity
    B. distance acuity
    C. depth perception
    D. peripheral vision

30. All of the following statements concerning body temperature in normal, healthy persons are correct EXCEPT: 30.____

    A. During the 24-hour day, the highest temperature is registered in the late afternoon or early evening
    B. During the 24-hour day, the lowest temperature is registered between 2 and 4 A. M., provided the person is not working on a night job

5 (#2)

- C. The more or less rhythmic rise and fall of body temperature is not established until adolescence
- D. In most normal people, the variations of temperature are so small that it is difficult to detect them without the use of a special thermometer

31. It has been found that, for most people, the BEST room temperature is about _____ °F with relative humidity of about _____.

    A. 70; 50%   B. 65; 40%   C. 68; 68%   D. 75; 75%

32. The MOST accurate of the following tuberculin tests is the

    A. Moro Test, using a tuberculin ointment
    B. Von Pirquet Test, applying tuberculin to the scratched skin
    C. Mantoux Test, injecting tuberculin preparation between the layers of the skin
    D. Patch Test, applying tuberculin ointment to the skin by gauze and adhesive plaster

33. All of the following statements concerning tetanus are true EXCEPT:

    A. Tetanus infection is likely only with puncture-type wounds
    B. Barnyard soil probably has the highest incidence of tetanus infestation
    C. Insignificant wounds often cause tetanus infection
    D. Immediate cleansing of a wound is a prime step in avoiding tetanus

34. All of the following are symptoms of a simple fracture of a bone EXCEPT

    A. deformity
    B. swelling
    C. a wound through the skin
    D. tenderness of the area to touch

35. A student who appears in the playground with an infected wound should be barred from physical activities PRIMARILY because

    A. other children may be infected
    B. a scab may be ruptured
    C. the spread of infection is likely
    D. pain may result

36. Traumatic shock following injury is directly attributable to

    A. pain
    B. loss of blood through external or internal bleeding
    C. psychological reactions
    D. failure of enough blood to circulate

37. Of the following, the substance that is NOT commonly used as an emetic is

    A. salt water   B. soap suds
    C. baking soda   D. ammonia water

38. All of the following statements concerning heat exhaustion are correct EXCEPT:

    A. In heat exhaustion, perspiration is usually profuse.
    B. Unconsciousness resulting from heat exhaustion is rare.

C. Salt tablets help to prevent heat exhaustion.
D. Body temperature rises rapidly.

39. Of the following, the gland MOST closely related to muscular efficiency is the   39.____

    A. adrenal   B. thyroid   C. gonads   D. pituitary

40. A deficiency of vitamin A in the diet may result in a condition known as   40.____

    A. beri-beri   B. scoliosis
    C. night blindness   D. scurvy

41. The condition in which a student is unable to focus both eyes on an object at the same time is termed   41.____

    A. strabismus   B. hyperopia
    C. emmetropia   D. scotoma

42. The *pressure point* MOST effective in controlling arterial bleeding of the forearm is located   42.____

    A. near the wrist
    B. near the elbow
    C. on the outer surface of the upper arm halfway between the shoulder and the elbow
    D. behind the inner end of the collarbone

43. The time interval between the entrance of infectious germs into the body and the appearance of the first symptoms is known as the _____ period.   43.____

    A. active   B. incubation   C. sequelae   D. prodromal

44. A condition which may result from a deficiency of vitamin C is known as   44.____

    A. beri-beri   B. rickets   C. scurvy   D. impetigo

45. Of the following, the contagious disease of the skin that the playground teacher should recognize in order to protect others is   45.____

    A. conjunctivitis   B. lordosis
    C. Osgood Schlatter's disease D. impetigo

46. Of the following, the symptom of heatstroke MOST frequently noted is   46.____

    A. an absence of perspiration
    B. mental confusion
    C. headache
    D. dilated pupils

47. A puncture wound is considered serious from the point of view that   47.____

    A. bleeding may be hard to stop
    B. injury to tissue may be extensive
    C. infection is likely to result
    D. multiple injury may result

48. Astigmatism is due PRIMARILY to

    A. a loss of elasticity in the lens
    B. the eyeballs' being too long
    C. an irregularity in the curvature of the eyeball
    D. an imbalance of eye muscles

49. With regard to respiration, it is CORRECT to state that

    A. in forced expiration, all of the air in the chest can be expelled
    B. the presence of carbon dioxide in the blood causes the brain area that controls breathing to act
    C. contraction of the muscles of the chest causes expiration
    D. every time one swallows, the windpipe is covered by the uvula

50. With regard to strains, all of the following are correct EXCEPT

    A. application of heat relieves the pain
    B. rubbing downward on the injured part aids the return flow of blood in the veins
    C. gentle massage helps loosen up the muscles
    D. rest is necessary

KEY (CORRECT ANSWERS)

1. D	11. B	21. B	31. A	41. A
2. B	12. B	22. D	32. C	42. D
3. B	13. B	23. C	33. A	43. B
4. C	14. C	24. B	34. C	44. C
5. D	15. B	25. B	35. C	45. D
6. D	16. D	26. A	36. D	46. A
7. C	17. A	27. C	37. D	47. C
8. C	18. A	28. B	38. D	48. C
9. D	19. D	29. B	39. A	49. B
10. A	20. B	30. C	40. C	50. B

TEST 3

DIRECTIONS: Each question or incomplete statement is followed by several suggested answers or completions. Select the one that BEST answers the question or completes the statement. *PRINT THE LETTER OF THE CORRECT ANSWER IN THE SPACE AT THE RIGHT.*

1. A short lapse of consciousness and a sudden momentary pause in conversation or movement is MOST suggestive of 1._____

    A. nephrosis
    B. autism
    C. Friedreich's ataxia
    D. petit mal seizure

2. Which one of the following diseases usually has a very poor prognosis? 2._____

    A. Hodgkin's disease
    B. Slipped epiphysis
    C. Cerebral palsy
    D. Eczema

3. Mononucleosis is an abnormal condition of the 3._____

    A. blood   B. liver   C. nerves   D. colon

4. Increased thirst, increased urination, loss of weight, and general fatigue are common symptoms of 4._____

    A. arthrogryposis
    B. diabetes
    C. hepatitis
    D. arthritis

5. Which one of the following is a disease of the ear? 5._____

    A. Ostitis
    B. Otitis
    C. Omphalitis
    D. Ophthalmia

6. Glomerulonephritis is a disease of the 6._____

    A. heart   B. stomach   C. kidney   D. larynx

7. Which one of the following is the disease that would MOST likely impair the ability to ambulate? 7._____

    A. Diabetes
    B. Colitis
    C. Bronchiectasis
    D. Spina bifida

8. The lay term *hunchback* is synonymous with 8._____

    A. kyphosis
    B. scoliosis
    C. torticollis
    D. spondylolisthesis

9. Which one of the following diseases involves a malformation of the heart? 9._____

    A. Hydrocele
    B. Tetralogy of Fallot
    C. Myasthenia gravis
    D. Lordosis

10. Of the following, the disease which would be included under the general classification *orthopedic* is 10._____

    A. lupus erythematosus
    B. lymphedema
    C. Osgood-Schlatter's
    D. opthalmospasm

85

11. Of the following cardiac classifications, the one the teacher would be LEAST likely to encounter is

    A. 4A
    B. 3C
    C. 4E
    D. 2C

12. A fusion operation upon the spine is often undertaken to correct

    A. pelvimetry
    B. paroxysm
    C. epiphysistis
    D. scoliosis

13. The treatment program for slipped epiphysis is MOST similar to the program for

    A. torticollis
    B. Perthe's disease
    C. polydactylism
    D. nephrosis

14. Which one of the following is MOST likely to be associated with production of large quantities of mucous?

    A. Kyphosis
    B. Bronchiectasis
    C. Lymphodenoma
    D. Thyroid deficiency

15. Poor bladder control is MOST frequently associated with

    A. rheumatic fever
    B. hemophilia
    C. club foot
    D. torticollis

16. Which one of the following conditions is caused by the inflammation of the lower part of the intestine?

    A. Pyelitis
    B. Transverse myelitis
    C. Regional ileitis
    D. Hepatitis

17. In contrast with former treatment methods that called for intramuscular injections, oral medication is now frequently provided for treating

    A. diabetes
    B. colitis
    C. thyroiditis
    D. myelitis

18. A cardiac child classified as 4E would be MOST apt to

    A. be placed in a health conservation class
    B. receive home instruction
    C. be placed in a regular class with limited physical activity
    D. be placed in a regular class following a short stay in a special class

19. An underweight child with a cardiac condition should be encouraged to

    A. add candy to his diet
    B. add carbohydrates such as bread and milk desserts to his diet
    C. maintain weight below normal since this insures a margin of safety should illness occur
    D. increase his intake of fluids and salt

20. When correctly used, the term *allergen* refers to

    A. a person who is allergic
    B. an antihistamine medication
    C. a substance which produces allergy
    D. the tendency to inherit an allergy

21. Which of the following is congenital?   21.____

    A. Meningitis   B. Gastroenteritis
    C. Chronic bronchitis   D. Osteogenesis imperfecta

22. Spasm is a common characteristic of   22.____

    A. slipped epiphysis   B. otitis
    C. muscular dystrophy   D. asthma

23. A disease usually characterized by frequent vomiting and cramps is   23.____

    A. colitis   B. bronchitis
    C. myocarditis   D. empyemia

24. A lateral curvature of the spine is characteristic of   24.____

    A. scoliosis   B. lordosis   C. hypnosis   D. stenosis

25. Which of the following is one of the GREAT dangers of many forms of anemia?   25.____

    A. Brain deterioration   B. Secondary infection
    C. Mental deficiency   D. Bleeding

26. Arteriosclerosis is a disturbance of the _____ system.   26.____

    A. skeletal   B. endocrine
    C. nervous   D. circulatory

27. Of the following disorders, which one is NOT a form of cerebral palsy?   27.____

    A. Little's disease   B. Athetosis
    C. Mitral's stenosis   D. Spastic paralysis

28. The chin is rotated away from the side of the short, prominent muscle; the head is tilted toward the affected side.   28.____
    These symptoms are characteristic of

    A. talipes   B. torticollis
    C. ligamentitis   D. bursitis

29. A patient designated by a physician as *Class IID* is suffering from   29.____

    A. diabetes   B. polio
    C. tuberculosis   D. heart disease

30. A dorsal curvature is generally referred to as   30.____

    A. lordosis   B. kyphosis   C. scoliosis   D. curatosis

31. A disease that usually occurs in overweight boys and girls between the ages of ten and thirteen years and is characterized by upper tibial epiphysitis is known as _____ disease.   31.____

    A. Pott's   B. Charcot-Tooth's
    C. Little's   D. Osgood-Schlatter's

32. A child whose walk is characterized by a scissors gait, with inward rotation and adduction of the legs, is probably suffering from

    A. Erb's palsy
    B. spasticity
    C. osteogenesis imperfecta
    D. spina bifida

33. Which of the following children will *generally* be placed in a regular class rather than in a health conservation class?

    A. Cardiopathic children
    B. Epileptic children
    C. Children with orthopedic handicaps
    D. Tuberculosis children

34. Which one of the following groups encompasses the LARGEST number of children? _____ children.

    A. Malnourished
    B. Crippled
    C. Cardiac
    D. Tuberculous

35. Rickets, a disease of nutrition manifested by disturbances in the general health and in the bones and joints, is caused by a lack of vitamin

    A. A
    B. B
    C. C
    D. D

36. Rheumatic fever

    A. most often strikes children between the ages of nine and ten
    B. is generally thought to be a streptococcal infection
    C. is generally accompanied by pain in the region of the heart
    D. is contagious

37. A young girl in your health conservation class has to have a blood transfusion every two weeks.
    She probably is suffering from

    A. gastritis
    B. hepatitis
    C. nephritis
    D. Cooley's disease

38. Differential diagnosis is MOST difficult in distinguishing between cases of

    A. poliomyelitis and meningitis
    B. aphasia and brain damage
    C. spasticity and athetosis
    D. leukemia and anemia

39. The MOST common complaint made by psychiatric patients is concerned with

    A. depression B. panic C. insomnia D. fatigue

40. The one of the following which is MOST likely to cause the reappearance in old age of a previously compensated neurosis is

    A. decrease in social status, loss of persons and possessions or presence of injuries and illnesses
    B. decrease in sensory and cognitive capacities resulting in poor reality testing

C. cerebro-arteriosclerosis or other cerebrovascular disturbance
D. decrease in financial resources, resulting in heightened anxiety

41. Infectious mononucleosis is also known as

   A. Hodgkin's disease
   B. glandular fever
   C. chorea
   D. bronchiectasis

42. Which one of the following is non-inflammatory?

   A. Cystitis   B. Nephritis   C. Nephrosis   D. Pyelitis

43. Idiopathic epilepsy may be BEST characterized as a condition which

   A. is of unknown origin
   B. is a result of some trauma
   C. is not amenable to treatment
   D. may be safely ignored

44. Which one of the following conditions is characterized by loss of weight, sleeplessness, irritability, and bulging eyes?

   A. Tuberculosis
   B. Overactive thyroid
   C. Myasthenia gravis
   D. Frederick's ataxia

45. Cardiac involvement may result from a previous acute, infectious disease. The disease referred to is

   A. streptococcus sore throat
   B. measles
   C. uremia
   D. enteric fever

46. A type of facial paralysis due to a neuritis of the facial nerve in the Fallopian canal is called

   A. Paget's disease
   B. Bell's palsy
   C. endocarditis
   D. encephalitis

47. A slipped epiphysis occurs MOST frequently in

   A. early adolescence
   B. late adolescence
   C. pre-adolescence
   D. early childhood

48. An electroencephalogram would NOT ordinarily be used in connection with

   A. epilepsy   B. ataxia   C. pyelitis   D. meningitis

49. Which of the following is characterized by lifeless muscle?

   A. Pott's disease
   B. Flaccid paralysis
   C. Scoliosis
   D. Colitis

50. Of the following diseases, the one that is NOT directly attributable to a specific vitamin deficiency is

   A. scurvy   B. beri-beri   C. tularemia   D. pellagra

KEY (CORRECT ANSWERS)

1. D	11. A	21. D	31. D	41. B
2. A	12. D	22. D	32. B	42. C
3. A	13. B	23. A	33. B	43. A
4. B	14. C	24. A	34. A	44. B
5. B	15. A	25. B	35. D	45. A
6. C	16. C	26. D	36. B	46. B
7. D	17. A	27. C	37. D	47. A
8. A	18. B	28. B	38. B	48. C
9. B	19. B	29. D	39. A	49. B
10. C	20. C	30. B	40. A	50. C

READING COMPREHENSION
UNDERSTANDING AND INTERPRETING WRITTEN MATERIAL
EXAMINATION SECTION
TEST 1

DIRECTIONS: Each question or incomplete statement is followed by several suggested answers or completions. Select the one that BEST answers the question or completes the statement. *PRINT THE LETTER OF THE CORRECT ANSWER IN THE SPACE AT THE RIGHT.*

Questions 1-4.

DIRECTIONS: Questions 1 through 4 are to be answered ONLY according to the information given in the following passage.

HANDLING HOSPITAL LAUNDRY

In a hospital, care must be taken when handling laundry in order to reduce the chance of germs spreading. There is always the possibility that dirty laundry will be carrying dangerous germs. To avoid catching germs when they are working with dirty laundry, laundry workers should be sure that any cuts or wounds they have are bandaged before they touch the dirty laundry. They should also be careful when handling this laundry not to rub their eyes, nose, or mouth. Just like all other hospital workers, laundry workers should also protect themselves against germs by washing and rinsing their hands thoroughly before eating meals and before leaving work at the end of the day.

To be sure that germs from dirty laundry do not pass onto clean laundry and thereby increase the danger to patients, clean and dirty laundry should not be handled near each other or by the same person. Special care also has to be taken with laundry that comes from a patient who has a dangerous, highly contagious disease so that as few people as possible come in direct contact with this laundry. Laundry from this patient, therefore, should be kept separate from other dirty laundry at all times.

1. According to the above passage, when working with dirty laundry, laundry workers should

    A. destroy laundry carrying dangerous germs
    B. have any cuts bandaged before touching the dirty laundry
    C. never touch the dirty laundry directly
    D. rub their eyes, nose, and mouth to protect them from germs

2. According to the above passage, all hospital workers should wash their hands thoroughly

    A. after eating meals to remove any trace of food from their hands
    B. at every opportunity to show good example to the patients
    C. before eating meals to protect themselves against germs
    D. before starting work in the morning to feel fresh and ready to do a good day's work

1.____

2.____

3. According to the above passage, the danger to patients will increase
   A. unless a worker handles dirty and clean laundry at the same time
   B. unless clean and dirty laundry are handled near each other
   C. when clean laundry is ironed frequently
   D. when germs pass from dirty laundry to clean laundry

4. According to the above passage, laundry from a patient with a dangerous, highly contagious disease should be
   A. given special care so that as few people as possible come in direct contact with it
   B. handled in the same way as any other dirty laundry
   C. washed by hand
   D. separated from the other dirty laundry just before it is washed

Questions 5-8.

DIRECTIONS: Questions 5 through 8 are to be answered ONLY according to the information given in the following passage.

MARKING PROCEDURES FOR PERSONAL WASH

As soon as a bundle of personal wash is brought into the laundry, it is taken to a marking section. Here an employee marks the individual pieces so that pieces following different courses through the laundry may be brought together when work upon them has been completed. The wash is identified either by visible markings, invisible markings, or by labels. Serial numbers and letters, often coded identifying the wash, are marked upon each article.

Visible markings should be placed on the concealed parts of the wash, such as trouser waistbands, either with a marking pencil or by a machine with a keyboard which looks like a typewriter. A similar machine is also used in laundries to mark pieces with invisible ink. These marks need not be concealed since they can be seen only under ultraviolet light. Labels with the markings on them, may be stapled or sewed onto each piece of wash. In addition to identifying, the marker has the task of listing, counting, and marking on a printed laundry list each piece in the bundle. After the wash has been marked, the marker then classifies the wash into groups that can be laundered together.

This is the only work done in the marking section.

5. According to the above passage, an IMPORTANT reason for placing identifying marks on personal wash is to
   A. keep a correct record of how many pounds of laundry are washed
   B. make sure that all the pieces in the bundle of laundry are washed together
   C. classify the pieces in the bundle according to the way they are washed
   D. make it possible to bring together later pieces that are washed separately

6. According to the above passage, in order to see a laundry mark made with invisible ink, it is necessary to
   A. use an ultraviolet light   B. wet it
   C. use a special machine   D. treat it with a mild acid

7. According to the above passage, an advantage of using invisible ink to mark laundry is that

   A. it is cheaper
   B. the mark can be made with an ordinary pencil
   C. the mark can be put any place on the wash and doesn't have to be hidden
   D. it takes less time to do the marking

8. According to the above passage, the marker does NOT

   A. put identifying marks on the wash
   B. sew small rips in torn wash
   C. check the number of pieces in each bundle of wash
   D. group the pieces of wash that can be laundered together

Questions 9-12.

DIRECTIONS: Questions 9 through 12 are to be answered ONLY according to the information given in the following passage.

THE HANDLING OF RAYON IN THE LAUNDRY

Rayon is an artificial fabric manufactured from wood pulp and short cotton fibres. It is extensively used in such items as shirtings, dress goods, and curtains, and may compose the entire fabric or simply be a part of the weave. While quite strong and substantial in its dry state, rayon is weak when wet and must, therefore, be handled with great care in the washing process. It should not be rubbed or stretched and should always be placed in nets to relieve as much strain as possible while in the washwheel. Rayon should preferably be washed in cold water with the proper materials for cold water washing. If there is any doubt as to whether a fabric is silk or rayon, a small thread or particle may be burnt. If it is silk, the threads will burn slowly and leave a small ball of ash at the end of the thread. Rayon, however, burns quickly and leaves no ash or telltale ball.

9. According to the above passage, rayon is made from a combination of _____ and _____

   A. wood; silk   B. wool; linen
   C. cotton; wood   D. silk; linen

10. According to the above passage, a manufacturer would probably NOT use rayon to make

    A. kitchen window curtains   B. dish towels
    C. nurses' uniforms   D. men's shirts

11. According to the above passage, the MAIN reason for putting rayon fabrics in a net when they are to be washed is that rayon is

    A. washable only in cold water
    B. a manufactured fabric
    C. easily stained by the materials from the washwheel
    D. not a strong material when wet

12. According to the above passage, threads of rayon burn _____ and leave _____ ash.   12.___

    A. slowly; no   B. fast; no
    C. slowly; a ball of   D. fast; a ball of

Questions 13-17.

DIRECTIONS: Questions 13 through 17 are to be answered ONLY according to the information given in the following paragraph.

REPORT FOR THE YEAR 2005 - LAUNDRY DIVISION

The Area A Central Laundry, which cost about 4½ million dollars with the equipment, was opened in December 2005, enabling the Department of Hospitals to close a number of out-of-date laundries in some Area A hospitals. The new Area A Central Laundry can now process 8,000 pounds of linen in an hour, or about 17½ million pounds a year. It has sufficient space for additional equipment to increase the capacity to 10,000 pounds per hour. The cost of processing laundry in 2004 at the old laundries was about twelve cents per pound. However, in 2005, the cost at the new laundry was about six cents per pound. Area A now does all the laundry for the municipal hospitals in that city and for the Area B Hospital Center.

During 2005, the laundries in Area C, D, E, and F Hospitals were also shut down and their work assigned to Area G laundry. About one-quarter of the original laundry staff was retained at each hospital to sort soiled linen and distribute clean linen — the other employees were reassigned to other laundries.

13. According to the above passage, can the new Area A Central Laundry do more than 8,000 pounds of linen an hour?   13.___

    A. Yes, if it gets more equipment
    B. Yes, only if it gets more space
    C. No, 8,000 pounds is the maximum capacity
    D. It is not possible to find this out from the passage

14. According to the above passage, the cost of processing laundry at the new Area A Laundry in 2005, as compared with the cost at the old laundries in 2004, was   14.___

    A. twice as much   B. about the same
    C. about half   D. only slightly less

15. According to the above passage, the cost of processing laundry in the new laundry was   15.___

    A. greater than at the old laundries
    B. equal to the cost at the laundries in Area C, D, E, and F Hospitals
    C. greater by 10,000 pounds per hour
    D. less by more than five cents per pound

16. According to the above passage, dirty linen from Area E Hospital is now laundred at the Area   16.___

    A. G laundry   B. A Central Laundry
    C. B Center Laundry   D. E Hospital

17. According to the above passage, what happened to the laundry workers at Area F Hospital when the laundry there was shut down? 17.____

    A. One-quarter of them went to Area A Central Laundry and the rest to the Area G laundry.
    B. Half of them were given jobs in other municipal departments and the rest were sent to other laundries.
    C. About three-quarters of them went to work at other laundries in the department.
    D. All of them were assigned to other hospital laundries to work on sorting and giving out laundry.

Questions 18-22.

DIRECTIONS: Questions 18 through 22 are to be answered ONLY according to the information given in the following paragraph.

The fact that your hospital has been ordered to make certain budgetary cutbacks has angered and frightened the community. A peaceful demonstration has been taking place for the last three days on hospital grounds. The group's leader has met with the hospital administrator; and although the meeting was amicable, nothing was resolved and the community still feels abused by the hospital, the health and hospitals corporation, and the city. Because you fear that the demonstration may become violent, you arrange to discuss first with the hospital administration and then with your staff what actions may become necessary.

18. Which of the following actions SHOULD be included in your preliminary plans? 18.____

    A. Notifying the media of a possible altercation at the hospital.
    B. Determining the location of the command post.
    C. Blocking all entrances and exits to the facility with furniture.
    D. Calling the administration and ordering them to leave the premises immediately.

19. Of the following, which is the MOST important topic you should discuss with your subordinates prior to the possible increased activity by the community? 19.____

    A. The nature of the group's complaints against the hospital and the city
    B. Your view on the hospital's position in this matter
    C. The need for self-control by all security personnel
    D. Hand-to-hand fighting techniques which may be necessary if the community group becomes violent

20. Assume that your concerns prove correct and the demonstration becomes less organized, less controlled, and potentially violent. 20.____
    As the supervisor of security personnel, your CHIEF responsibility is to

    A. join your men in quelling any disturbance
    B. maintain a clearly defined chain of command so that orders remain clear and concise
    C. prevent the demonstration's leaders from entering the hospital administration building so that hospital routines may continue without interruption
    D. meet with demonstration leaders as soon as possible

21. The one of the following choices that contains only the MOST important items of information a security officer should transmit to his hospital administrator in the situation described above is the

    A. approximate size of the group of demonstrators, the security measures already taken, and the number of officers on duty
    B. number of available parking spaces, the demands of the demonstrators, and the names of community leaders seen
    C. number of officers on leave, the number of patients in the hospital, and the approximate size of the group of demonstrators
    D. number of officers on leave, the demands of the demonstrators, and the number of plant maintenance staff on duty

22. Of the following, the area whose security is LEAST important to protect during the demonstrations is the

    A. pharmacy
    B. patients' accounts office
    C. pathology laboratory
    D. linen storage rooms

Questions 23-25.

DIRECTIONS: Questions 23 through 25 are to be answered ONLY according to the information given in the following statement.

When a voluntary hospital admits a Blue Cross subscriber who has been referred from a city hospital, a concurrent submission of the case shall be made by it to both Blue Cross and the city Investigator who routinely visits the voluntary hospital. This procedure will be advantageous to both the voluntary hospital and the city since the hospital would be notified immediately of the ability of the city to reimburse should Blue Cross coverage be inapplicable or insufficient. Furthermore, the city will be able to assure itself of potential State Aid for those cases for whom it may have to assume some responsibility. Necessary time limits to process applications for State Aid can also be made if this referral is concurrent, such as for state charges and relief clients, who are frequently Blue Cross members. This investigation can best be conducted by the city staff assigned to the voluntary hospital, rather than by the staff in the referring Municipal hospital.

23. According to the above statement, one responsibility of a voluntary hospital with respect to an admission who is a Blue Cross subscriber is to

    A. get the city to reimburse its fair share if Blue Cross coverage is inapplicable or insufficient
    B. refer the case to the city hospital for possible collection of State Aid
    C. submit the case concurrently to both Blue Cross and the city Investigator
    D. submit the case to the city investigator if the patient has been referred by a city hospital

24. According to the above statement, it is NOT an advantage of the procedure described that the

    A. city can make sure of getting possible State Aid for those cases for whom it may be partly responsible
    B. cost of caring for the cases referred to will be shared by Blue Cross, the Voluntary hospital, the city, and the State
    C. needed time limits to handle State Aid applications can be made
    D. Voluntary hospitals will know immediately if the city will pay for its referrals who do not have enough Blue Cross coverage

25. According to the above statement, the investigation referred to can be carried out MOST advantageously by the   25._____

    A. city investigator who routinely visits the Voluntary hospital
    B. city staff assigned to the hospital that admitted the patient
    C. staff of the hospital that referred the patient
    D. staff of the Voluntary hospital that accepted the referral

---

KEY (CORRECT ANSWERS)

1.	B	11.	D
2.	C	12.	B
3.	D	13.	A
4.	A	14.	C
5.	D	15.	D
6.	A	16.	A
7.	C	17.	C
8.	B	18.	B
9.	C	19.	C
10.	B	20.	B

21. A
22. D
23. D
24. B
25. B

TEST 2

DIRECTIONS: Each question consists of a statement. You are to indicate whether the statement is TRUE (T) or FALSE (F). *PRINT THE LETTER OF THE CORRECT ANSWER IN THE SPACE AT THE RIGHT.*

Questions 1-9.

DIRECTIONS: Questions 1 through 9 are to be answered SOLELY on the basis of the information contained in the following passage.

All deaths must be reported to the Department of Health by the licensed physician in attendance at the time of death if death is from natural causes and does not occur in a hospital, or by the person in charge of a hospital if the death occurs there from natural causes, or by the office of the chief medical examiner if the death is apparently from other than natural causes such as violence or suicide. The physician in attendance or the person in charge of a hospital must file a death certificate accompanied by a confidential medical report. The office of the medical examiner files only a death certificate. These papers should be filed within twenty-four hours after death or finding of the remains, with the office of the Department of Health in the borough in which the death occurs or in which the remains are found. However, this requirement is also considered fulfilled if such papers are delivered immediately upon demand and within the twenty-four hours either to a funeral director or undertaker authorized to take charge of the remains or to the city superintendent of mortuaries for those cases in which the remains are to be buried in the city cemetery. These persons receiving the papers must then file the certificates and confidential report with the Department of Health within 48 hours following death or the finding of the remains.

1. A death from heart disease at home must be reported to the Department of Health by the licensed physician in attendance at the time of death.   1.____

2. All deaths outside a hospital must be reported to the Department of Health by the physician in attendance.   2.____

3. The Police Department reports all violent deaths to the Department of Health.   3.____

4. When the death is a suicide, a confidential medical report is filed by the medical examiner.   4.____

5. If a person dies in a hospital from other than natural causes, the death certificate must be filed by the office of the medical examiner.   5.____

6. If a person who lives in Brooklyn dies in Manhattan, the death certificate must be filed in Manhattan.   6.____

7. The physician in attendance who is required to file a death certificate must do so within 24 hours after the death.   7.____

8. The death certificate may also be delivered to an authorized undertaker instead of filing it directly with the Department of Health.   8.____

9. The authorized funeral director who has the death certificate must file it with the Department of Health within twenty-four hours after he has received it.   9.____

Questions 10-22.

DIRECTIONS: Questions 10 through 22 are to be answered SOLELY on the basis of the information contained in the following paragraph.

THE HUMAN BODY

The vertebrae of the spinal column all have the same general shape in that each has a thick body of bone in front, from the sides of which two lighter extensions of bone pass backwards and around to join each other, thus forming an opening in the center. These openings, placed in line with each other as in an intact spinal column, help form the spinal canal which encloses and protects the spinal cord. Cartilage plates between the bodies of the upper twenty-four vertebrae permit considerable movement of the vertebrae and cushion the shock of falling. The sternum is a long, flat bone forming the middle part of the chest's front wall. The upper end of the sternum is a long, flat bone forming the middle part of the chest's front wall. The upper end of the sternum supports the collarbones, and most of the ribs on each side of the chest are attached to the sternum by means of cartilage. Each of the twelve ribs on each side of the chest's bony framework is joined to the spinal column by a movable joint. The first seven ribs, on each side, called true ribs, are joined in front to the sternum by cartilage, and the next three, called false ribs, are each joined similarly to the rib immediately above. The lowest two, called floating ribs, are not fastened at all by their front ends. The pelvis, a basin-shaped ring of bones, is located between the movable vertebrae of the spinal column, which it supports, and the lower limbs, on which it rests. The pelvis, forming the floor of the abdominal cavity and providing deep pockets into which the heads of the thighbones fit, consists of four bones: the sacrum and coccyx behind, and the two hip bones at the sides and front.

10. The vertebrae have a bony part only in the front.   10.____

11. The spinal cord passes through the openings in the center of the vertebrae.   11.____

12. The total number of ribs in the body is 24.   12.____

13. The spinal cord is made up of the openings in the vertebrae.   13.____

14. The shock of falling is eased by cartilage plates between the vertebrae.   14.____

15. The sternum is at the rear of the chest cavity.   15.____

16. The collarbones are supported by the top part of the sternum.   16.____

17. All the ribs are joined in the front to the sternum by cartilage.   17.____

18. The floating ribs are not fastened to the spinal column at all.   18.____

19. The pelvis is a bony structure.   19.____

20. The hip bones are a part of the pelvis.   20.____

21. The pelvis is at the bottom of the abdominal cavity.   21.____

Questions 22-26.

DIRECTIONS: Questions 22 through 26 are to be answered SOLELY on the basis of the information contained in the following paragraph.

RELEASE OF HUMAN REMAINS FROM CITY MORTUARY

When human remains which have been removed to the city mortuary are subsequently claimed, the superintendent of city mortuaries shall deliver the remains, on demand, only to a funeral director or undertaker. The latter must submit a written statement that he or the funeral establishment with which he is associated has been employed by the next of kin, legal representative, or, in the absence of arrangements by such next of kin or legal representative, by a friend of the deceased. Together with the remains, the superintendent shall deliver the certificate of death or fetal death and confidential medical report, if any, or, any permit issued by the Department authorizing burial in the city cemetery. No burial permit may be issued unless the certificate of death has been filed with the Department of Health.

22. To secure the release of human remains from the city mortuary, the next of kin must advise the mortuaries superintendent by telephone of the name of the undertaker. 22.___

23. The superintendent of city mortuaries cannot release a body directly to the next of kin. 23.___

24. If there is a confidential medical report, the superintendent of city mortuaries is supposed to deliver this with the body to the person authorized to receive the body. 24.___

25. The permit for burial in the city cemetery is shown to the duly employed undertaker, but is kept by the superintendent of city mortuaries. 25.___

26. If a certificate of death has not been filed with the Department of Health, no burial permit may be issued. 26.___

Questions 27-30.

DIRECTIONS: Questions 27 through 30 are to be answered SOLELY on the basis of the information given in this paragraph.

CARBON MONOXIDE GAS

Carbon monoxide is a deadly gas from the effects of which no one is immune. Any person's strength will be cut down considerably by breathing this gas, even though he does not take in enough to overcome him. Wearing a handkerchief tied around the nose and mouth offers some protection against the irritating fumes of ordinary smoke, but many people have died convinced that a handkerchief will stop carbon monoxide. Any person entering a room filled with this deadly gas should wear a mask equipped with an air hose, or even better, an oxygen breathing apparatus.

27. Some people get no ill effects from carbon monoxide gas until they are overcome. 27.___

28. A person can die from breathing carbon monoxide gas. 28.___

29. A handkerchief around the mouth and nose gives some protection against the effects of ordinary smoke.   29._____

30. It is better for a person entering a room filled with carbon monoxide to wear a mask equipped with an air hose than an oxygen breathing apparatus.   30._____

KEY (CORRECT ANSWERS)

1.	T	16.	T
2.	F	17.	F
3.	F	18.	F
4.	F	19.	T
5.	T	20.	T
6.	T	21.	T
7.	T	22.	F
8.	T	23.	T
9.	F	24.	T
10.	F	25.	F
11.	T	26.	T
12.	T	27.	F
13.	T	28.	T
14.	T	29.	T
15.	F	30.	F

CLERICAL ABILITIES TEST

Clerical aptitude involves the ability to perceive pertinent detail in verbal or tabular material, to observe differences in copy, to proofread words and numbers, and to avoid perceptual errors in arithmetic computation.

NATURE OF THE TEST

Four types of clerical aptitude questions are presented in the Clerical Abilities Test. There are 120 questions with a short time limit. The test contains 30 questions on name and number checking, 30 on the arrangement of names in correct alphabetical order, 30 on simple arithmetic, and 30 on inspecting groups of letters and numbers. The questions have been arranged in groups or cycles of five questions of each type. The Clerical Abilities Test is primarily a test of speed in carrying out relatively simple clerical tasks. While accuracy on these tasks is important and will be taken into account in the scoring, experience has shown that many persons are so concerned about accuracy that they do the test more slowly than they should. Competitors should be cautioned that speed as well as accuracy is important to achieve a good score.

HOW THE TEST IS ADMINISTERED

Each competitor should be given a copy of the test booklet with sample questions on the cover page, an answer sheet, and a medium No. 2 pencil. Ten minutes are allowed to study the directions and sample questions and to answer the questions in the proper boxes on the two pages.
The separate answer sheet should be used for the test proper. Fifteen minutes are allowed for the test.

HOW THE TEST IS SCORED

The correct answers should be counted and recorded. The number of incorrect answers must also be counted because one-fourth of the number of incorrect answers is subtracted from the number of right answers. An omission is considered as neither a right nor a wrong answer. The score on this test is the number of right answers minus one-fourth of the number of wrong answers (fractions of one-half or less are dropped). For example, if an applicant had answered 89 questions correctly and 10 questions incorrectly, and had omitted 1 question, his score would be 87.

EXAMINATION SECTION

DIRECTIONS: This test contains four kinds of questions. There are some of each kind on each page in the booklet. The time limit for the test will be announced by the examiner.
Use the special pencil furnished by the examiner in marking your answers on the separate answer sheet. For each question, there are five suggested answers. Decide which answer is correct, find the number of the question on the answer sheet, and make a solid black mark between the dotted lines just below the letter of your answer. If you wish to change your answer, erase the first mark completely, do not merely cross it out.

SAMPLE QUESTIONS

In each line across the page there are three names or numbers that are much alike. Compare the three names or numbers and decide which ones are exactly alike. On the Sample Answer Sheet at the right, mark the answer
  A. if ALL THREE names or numbers are exactly ALIKE
  B. if only the FIRST and SECOND names or numbers are exactly ALIKE
  C. if only the FIRST and THIRD names or numbers are exactly ALIKE
  D. if only the SECOND and THIRD names or numbers are exactly ALIKE
  E. if ALL THREE names or numbers are DIFFERENT

I.	Davis Hazen	David Hozen	David Hazen
II.	Lois Appel	Lois Appel	Lois Apfel
III.	June Allan	Jane Allan	Jane Allan
IV.	10235	10235	10235
V.	32614	32164	32614

It will be to your advantage to learn what A, B, C, D, and E stand for. If you finish the sample questions before you are told to turn to the test, study them.

In the next group of sample questions, there is a name in a box at the left, and four other names in alphabetical order at the right. Find the correct space for the boxed name so that it will be in alphabetical order with the others, and mark the letter of that space as your answer.

VI. | Jones, Jane |

A. →
   Goodyear, G.L.
B. →
   Haddon, Harry
C. →
   Jackson, Mary
D. →
   Jenkins, William
E. →

VII. | Kessler, Neilson |

A. →
   Kessel, Carl
B. →
   Kessinger, D.J.
C. →
   Kessler, Karl
D. →
   Kessner, Lewis
E. →

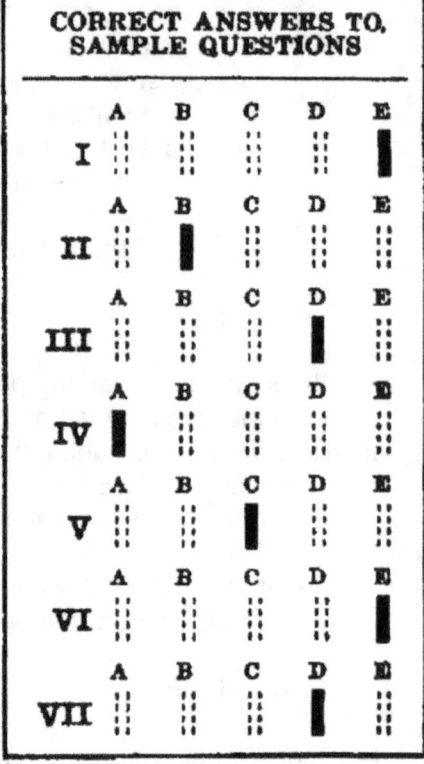

DIRECTIONS: In the following questions, complete the equation and find your answer among the list of suggested answers. Mark the Sample Answer Sheet A, B, C, or D for the answer you obtained; or if your answer is not among these, mark E for that question.

VIII. Add: 22
           +33

   A. 44   B. 45   C. 54   D. 55   E. None of these

IX. Subtract: 24
             - 3

   A. 20   B. 21   C. 27   D. 29   E. None of these

X. Multiply: 25
             x 5

   A. 100   B. 115   C. 125   D. 135   E. None of these

XI. Divide: 6/126̄

    A. 20   B. 22   C. 24   D. 26   E. None of these

DIRECTIONS: There is one set of suggested answers for the next group of sample questions. Do not try to memorize these answers, because there will be a different set on each age in the test.

    To find the answer to a question, find which suggested answer contains numbers and letters, all of which appear in the question. If no suggested answer fits, mark E for that question.

XII. 8 N K 9 G T 4 6

XIII. T 9 7 Z 6 L 3 K

XIV. Z 7 G K 3 9 8 N

XV. 3 K 9 4 6 G Z L

XVI. Z N 7 3 8 K T 9

Suggested Answers
A = 7, 9, G, K
B = 8, 9, T, Z
C = 6, 7, K, Z
D = 6, 8, G, T
E = None of the above

    After you have marked your answers to all the questions on the Sample Answer Sheets on this page and on the front page of the booklet, check them with the answers in the boxes marked Correct Answers To Sample Questions.

Questions 1-5.

In Questions 1 through 5, compare the three names or numbers, and mark
    A. if ALL THREE names or numbers are exactly ALIKE
    B. if only the FIRST and SECOND names or numbers are exactly ALIKE
    C. if only the FIRST and THIRD names or numbers are exactly ALIKE
    D. if only the SECOND and THIRD names or numbers are exactly ALIKE
    E. if ALL THREE names or numbers are DIFFERENT

1. 5261383   5261383   5261338

2. 8125690   8126690   8125609

3. W.E. Johnston   W.E. Johnson   W.E. Johnson

4. Vergil L. Muller   Vergil L. Muller   Vergil L. Muller

5. Atherton R. Warde   Asheton R. Warde   Atherton P. Warde

Questions 6-10.

In Questions 6 through 10, find the correct place for the name in the box

6. | Hackett, Gerald |

    A. →
        Habert, James
    B. →
        Hachett, J.J.
    C. →
        Hachetts, K. Larson
    D. →
        Hachettson, Leroy
    E. →

7. | Margenroth, Alvin |

    A. →
        Margeroth, Albert
    B. →
        Margestein, Dan
    C. →
        Margestein, David
    D. →
        Margue, Edgar
    E. →

8. | Bobbitt, Olivier E. |

    A. →
        Bobbitt, D. Olivier
    B. →
        Bobbitt, Olivia B
    C. →
        Bobbitt, Olivia H.
    D. →
        Bobbitt, R. Olivia
    E. →

9. | Mosley, Werner |

    A. →
        Mosely, Albert J.
    B. →
        Mosley, Alvin
    C. →
        Mosley, S.M.
    D. →
        Mozley, Vinson N.
    E. →

10. | Youmuns, Frank L. | A. →
                            Youmons, Frank G.
                         B. →
                            Youmons, Frank H.
                         C. →
                            Youmons, Frank K.
                         D. →
                            Youmons, Frank M.
                         E. →

Questions 11-15.

11. Add: 43
         +32

    A. 55   B. 65   C. 66   D. 75   E. None of these

12. Subtract: 83
              - 4

    A. 73   B. 79   C. 80   D. 89   E. None of these

13. Multiply: 41
              x 7

    A. 281   B. 287   C. 291   D. 297   E. None of these

14. Divide: 6/306

    A. 44   B. 51   C. 52   D. 60   E. None of these

15. Add: 37
         +15

    A. 42   B. 52   C. 53   D. 62   E. None of these

Questions 16-20.

In Questions 16 through 20, find which one of the suggested answers appears in that question.

16. 6 2 5 K 4 P T G

17. L 4 7 2 T 6 V K

18. 3 5 4 L 9 V T G

19. G 4 K 7 L 3 5 Z

SUGGESTED ANSWERS
A = 4, 5, K, T
B = 4, 7, G, K
C = 2, 5, G, L
D = 2, 7, L, T
E = None of the above

20. 4 K 2 9 N 5 T G

Questions 21-25.

In Questions 21 through 25, compare the three names or numbers, and mark
    A. if ALL THREE names or numbers are exactly ALIKE
    B. if only the FIRST and SECOND names or numbers are exactly ALIKE
    C. if only the FIRST and THIRD names or numbers are exactly ALIKE
    D. if only the SECOND and THIRD names or numbers are exactly ALIKE
    E. if ALL THREE names or numbers are DIFFERENT

21. 2395890   2395890   2395890

22. 1926341   1926347   1926314

23. E. Owens McVey   E. Owen McVey   E. Owen McVay

24. Emily Neal Rouse   Emily Neal Rowse   Emily Neal Rowse

25. H. Merritt Audubon   H. Merriott Audubon H. Merritt Audubon

Questions 26-30.

In Questions 26 through 30, find the correct place for the name in the box.

26. | Watters, N.O. |
    A. →
        Waters, Charles L.
    B. →
        Waterson, Nina P.
    C. →
        Watson, Nora J.
    D. →
        Wattwood, Paul A.
    E. →

27. | Johnston, Edward |
    A. →
        Johnston, Edgar R.
    B. →
        Johnston, Edmond
    C. →
        Johnston, Edmund
    D. →
        Johnstone, Edmund A.
    E. →

28. Rensch, Adeline

A. →
   Ramsay, Amos
B. →
   Remschel, Augusta
C. →
   Renshaw, Austin
D. →
   Rentzel, Becky
E. →

29. Schnyder, Maurice

A. →
   Schneider, Martin
B. →
   Schneider, Mertens
C. →
   Schnyder, Newman
D. →
   Schreibner, Norman
E. →

30. Freedenburg, C. Erma

A. →
   Freedenberg, Emerson
B. →
   Freedenberg, Erma
C. →
   Freedenberg, Erma E.
D. →
   Freedinberg, Erma F.
E. →

Questions 31-35.

31. Subtract: 68
              - 47

    A. 10   B. 11   C. 20   D. 22   E. None of these

32. Multiply: 50
              x 8

    A. 400   B. 408   C. 450   D. 458   E. None of these

33. Divide: 9/180

    A. 20   B. 29   C. 30   D. 39   E. None of these

34. Add: 78
           + 63

    A. 131   B. 140   C. 141   D. 151   E. None of these

35. Add: 89
      - 70

   A. 9   B. 18   C. 19   D. 29   E. None of these

Questions 36-40.

In Questions 36 through 40, find which one of the suggested answers appears in that question.

36. 9 G Z 3 L 4 6 N

37. L 5 N K 4 3 9 V

38. 8 2 V P 9 L Z 5

39. V P 9 Z 5 L 8 7

40. 5 T 8 N 2 9 V L

SUGGESTED ANSWERS
A = 4, 9, L, V
B = 4, 5, N, Z
C = 5, 8, L, Z
D = 8, 9, N, V
E = None of the above

Questions 41-45.

In Questions 41 through 45, compare the three names or numbers, and mark
   A. if ALL THREE names or numbers are exactly ALIKE
   B. if only the FIRST and SECOND names or numbers are exactly ALIKE
   C. if only the FIRST and THIRD names or numbers are exactly ALIKE
   D. if only the SECOND and THIRD names or numbers are exactly ALIKE
   E. if ALL THREE names or numbers are DIFFERENT

41. 6219354	621354	6219354
42. 2312793	2312793	2312793
43. 1065407	1065407	1065047
44. Francis Ransdell	Frances Ramsdell	Francis Ramsdell
45. Cornelius Detwiler	Cornelius Detwiler	Cornelius Detwiler

Questions 46-50.

In Questions 46 through 50, find the correct place for the name in the box.

46. [DeMattia, Jessica]

A. →
DeLong, Jesse
B. →
DeMatteo, Jessie
C. →
Derby, Jessie S.
D. →
DeShazo, L.M.
E. →

47. [Theriault, Louis]

A. →
Therien, Annette
B. →
Therien, Elaine
C. →
Thibeault, Gerald
D. →
Thiebeault, Pierre
E. →

48. [Gaston, M. Hubert]

A. →
Gaston, Dorothy M.
B. →
Gaston, Henry N.
C. →
Gaston, Isabel
D. →
Gaston, M. Melvin
E. →

49. [SanMiguel, Carlos]

A. →
SanLuis, Juana
B. →
Santilli, Laura
C. →
Stinnett, Nellie
D. →
Stoddard, Victor
E. →

50. | DeLaTour, Hall F. |

A. →
   DeLargy, Harold
B. →
   DeLathouder, Hilda
C. →
   Lathrop, Hillary
D. →
   LaTour, Hulbert E.
E. →

Questions 51-55.

51. Multiply: 62
    x 5

    A. 300   B. 310   C. 315   D. 360   E. None of these

52. Divide: 3/153

    A. 41   B. 43   C. 51   D. 53   E. None of these

53. Add: 47
    +21

    A. 58   B. 59   C. 67   D. 68   E. None of these

54. Subtract: 87
    - 42

    A. 34   B. 35   C. 44   D. 45   E. None of these

55. Multiply: 37
    x 3

    A. 91   B. 101   C. 104   D. 114   E. None of these

Questions 56-60.

For Questions 56 through 60, find which one of the suggested answers appears in that question.

56. N 5 4 7 T K 3 Z

57. 8 5 3 V L 2 Z N

58. 7 2 5 N 9 K L V

59. 9 8 L 2 5 Z K V

60. Z 6 5 V 9 3 P N

SUGGESTED ANSWERS
A = 3, 8, K, N
B = 5, 8, N, V
C = 3, 9, V, Z
D = 5, 9, K, Z
E = None of the above

Questions 61-65.

In Questions 61 through 65, compare the three names or numbers, and mark
- A. if ALL THREE names or numbers are exactly ALIKE
- B. if only the FIRST and SECOND names or numbers are exactly ALIKE
- C. if only the FIRST and THIRD names or numbers are exactly ALIKE
- D. if only the SECOND and THIRD names or numbers are exactly ALIKE
- E. if ALL THREE names or numbers are DIFFERENT

61. 6452054   6452654   6452054

62. 8501268   8501268   8501286

63. Ella Burk Newham   Ella Burk Newnham   Elena Burk Newnham

64. Jno. K. Ravencroft   Jno. H. Ravencroft   Jno. H. Ravencoft

65. Martin Wills Pullen Martin Wills Pulen   Martin Wills Pullen

Questions 66-70.

In Questions 66 through 70, find the correct place for the name in the box.

66. | O'Bannon, M.J. |
- A. →
  O'Beirne, B.B.
- B. →
  Oberlin, E.L.
- C. →
  Oberneir, L.P.
- D. →
  O'Brian, S.F.
- E. →

67. | Entsminger, Jacob |
- A. →
  Ensminger, J.
- B. →
  Entsminger, J.A.
- C. →
  Entsminger, Jack
- D. →
  Entsminger, James
- E. →

68. Iacone, Pete R.

A. →
Iacone, Pedro
B. →
Iacone, Pedro M.
C. →
Iacone, Peter F.
D. →
Iascone, Peter W.
E. →

69. Sheppard, Gladys

A. →
Shepard, Dwight
B. →
Shepard, F.H.
C. →
Shephard, Louise
D. →
Shepperd, Stella
E. →

70. Thackton, Melvin T.

A. →
Thackston, Milton G.
B. →
Thackston, Milton W.
C. →
Thackston, Theodore
D. →
Thackston, Thomas G.
E. →

Questions 71-75.

71. Divide: 7/357

    A. 51   B. 52   C. 53   D. 54   E. None of these

72. Add: 58
         +27

    A. 75   B. 84   C. 85   D. 95   E. None of these

73. Subtract: 86
              - 57

    A. 18   B. 29   C. 38   D. 39   E. None of these

74. Multiply: 68
             x 4

    A. 242   B. 264   C. 272   D. 274   E. None of these

75. Divide: 9/639̄

    A. 71   B. 73   C. 81   D. 83   E. None of these

Questions 76-80.

For Questions 76 through 80, find which one of the suggested answers appears in that question.

76. 6 Z T N 8 7 4 V

77. V 7 8 6 N 5 P L

78. N 7 P V 8 4 2 L

79. 7 8 G 4 3 V L T

80. 4 8 G 2 T N 6 L

SUGGESTED ANSWERS
A = 2, 7, L, N
B = 2, 8, T, V
C = 6, 8, L, T
D = 6, 7, N, V
E = None of the above

Questions 81-85.

In Questions 81 through 85, compare the three names or numbers, and mark
   A. if ALL THREE names or numbers are exactly ALIKE
   B. if only the FIRST and SECOND names or numbers are exactly ALIKE
   C. if only the FIRST and THIRD names or numbers are exactly ALIKE
   D. if only the SECOND and THIRD names or numbers are exactly ALIKE
   E. if ALL THREE names or numbers are DIFFERENT

81.	3457988	3457986	3457986
82.	4695682	4695862	4695682
83.	Stricklund Kanedy	Stricklund Kanedy	Stricklund Kanedy
84.	Joy Harbor Witner	Joy Harloe Witner	Joy Harloe Witner
85.	R.M.O. Uberroth	R.M.O. Uberroth	R.N.O. Uberroth

Questions 86-90.

In Questions 86 through 90, find the correct place for the name in the box.

86. Dunlavey, M. Hilary

A. →
Dunleavy, Hilary G.
B. →
Dunleavy, Hilary K.
C. →
Dunleavy, Hilary S.
D. →
Dunleavy, Hilery W.
E. →

87. Yarbrough, Maria

A. →
Yabroudy, Margy
B. →
Yarboro, Marie
C. →
Yarborough, Marina
D. →
Yarborough, Mary
E. →

88. Prouty, Martha

A. →
Proutey, Margaret
B. →
Proutey, Maude
C. →
Prouty, Myra
D. →
Prouty, Naomi
E. →

89. Pawlowicz, Ruth M.

A. →
Pawalek, Edward
B. →
Pawelek, Flora G.
C. →
Pawlowski, Joan M.
D. →
Pawtowski, Wanda
E. →

90. Vanstory, George

A. → Vanover, Eva
B. → VanSwinderen, Floyd
C. → VanSyckle, Harry
D. → Vanture, Laurence
E. →

Questions 91-95

91. Add: 28
    +35

    A. 53   B. 62   C. 64   D. 73   E. None of these

92. Subtract: 78
    -69

    A. 7   B. 8   C. 18   D. 19   E. None of these

93. Multiply: 86
    x 6

    A. 492   B. 506   C. 516   D. 526   E. None of these

94. Divide: 8/648

    A. 71   B. 76   C. 81   D. 89   E. None of these

95. Add: 97
    +34

    A. 131   B. 132   C. 140   D. 141   E. None of these

Questions 96-100.

For Questions 96 through 100, find which one of the suggested answers appears in that question.

96. V 5 7 Z N 9 4 T

97. 4 6 P T 2 N K 9

98. 6 4 N 2 P 8 Z K

99. 7 P 5 2 4 N K T

100. K T 8 5 4 N 2 P

SUGGESTED ANSWERS
A = 2, 5, N, Z
B = 4, 5, N, P
C = 2, 9, P, T
D = 4, 9, T, Z
E = None of the above

Questions 101-105.

In Questions 101 through 105, compare the three names or numbers, and mark
    A. if ALL THREE names or numbers are exactly ALIKE
    B. if only the FIRST and SECOND names or numbers are exactly ALIKE
    C. if only the FIRST and THIRD names or numbers are exactly ALIKE
    D. if only the SECOND and THIRD names or numbers are exactly ALIKE
    E. if ALL THREE names or numbers are DIFFERENT

101. 1592514   1592574   1592574

102. 2010202   2010202   2010220

103. 6177396   6177936   6177396

104. Drusilla S. Ridgeley   Drusilla S. Ridgeley   Drusilla S. Ridgeley

105. Andrei I. Toumantzev   Andrei I. Tourmantzev   Andrei I. Toumantzov

Questions 106-110.

In Questions 106 through 110, find the correct place for the name in the box.

106. | Fitzsimmons, Hugh |
    A. →
        Fitts, Harold
    B. →
        Fitzgerald, June
    C. →
        FitzGibbon, Junius
    D. →
        FitzSimons, Martin
    E. →

107. | D'Amato, Vincent |
    A. →
        Daly, Steven
    B. →
        D'Amboise, S. Vincent
    C. →
        Daniel, Vail
    D. →
        DeAlba, Valentina
    E. →

108. Schaeffer, Roger D.

A. →
Schaffert, Evelyn M.
B. →
Schaffner, Margaret M.
C. →
Schafhirt, Milton G.
D. →
Shafer, Richard E.
E. →

109. White-Lewis, Cecil

A. →
Whitelaw, Cordelia
B. →
White-Leigh, Nancy
C. →
Whitely, Rodney
D. →
Whitlock, Warren
E. →

110. VanDerHeggen, Don

A. →
VanDemark, Doris
B. →
Vandenberg, H.E.
C. →
VanDercook, Marie
D. →
vanderLinden, Robert
E. →

Questions 111-115.

111. Add: 75
     +49

    A. 124   B. 125   C. 134   D. 225   E. None of these

112. Subtract: 69
              - 45

    A. 14   B. 23   C. 24   D. 26   E. None of these

113. Multiply: 36
              x 8

    A. 246   B. 262   C. 288   D. 368   E. None of these

114. Divide: 8/328̄

    A. 31   B. 41   C. 42   D. 48   E. None of these

115. Multiply: 58
             x 9

    A. 472   B. 513   C. 521   D. 522   E. None of these

Questions 116-120.

For Questions 116 through 120, find which one of the suggested answers appears in that question.

116. Z 3 N P G 5 4 2

117. 6 N 2 8 G 4 P T

118. 6 N 4 T V G 8 2

119. T 3 P 4 N 8 G 2

120. 6 7 K G N 2 L 5

SUGGESTED ANSWERS:
A = 2, 3, G, N
B = 2, 6, N, T
C = 3, 4, G, K
D = 4, 6, K, T
E = None of the above

KEY (CORRECT ANSWERS)

1.	B	21.	A	41.	A	61.	C	81.	D	101.	D
2.	E	22.	E	42.	A	62.	B	82.	C	102.	B
3.	D	23.	E	43.	B	63.	E	83.	A	103.	C
4.	A	24.	D	44.	E	64.	E	84.	D	104.	A
5.	E	25.	C	45.	A	65.	C	85.	B	105.	E
6.	E	26.	D	46.	C	66.	A	86.	A	106.	D
7.	A	27.	D	47.	A	667.	D	87.	E	107.	B
8.	D	28.	C	48.	D	68.	C	88.	C	108.	A
9.	B	29.	C	49.	B	69.	D	89.	C	109.	C
10.	E	30.	D	50.	C	70.	E	90.	B	110.	D
11.	D	31.	E	51.	B	71.	A	91.	E	111.	A
12.	B	32.	A	52.	C	72.	C	92.	E	112.	C
13.	B	33.	A	53.	D	73.	B	93.	C	113.	C
14.	B	34.	C	54.	D	74.	C	94.	C	114.	B
15.	B	35.	C	55.	E	75.	A	95.	A	115.	D
16.	A	36.	E	56.	E	76.	D	96.	D	116.	A
17.	D	37.	A	57.	B	77.	D	97.	C	117.	B
18.	E	38.	C	58.	E	78.	A	98.	E	118.	B
19.	B	39.	C	59.	D	79.	E	99.	B	119.	A
20.	A	40.	D	60.	C	80.	C	100.	B	120.	E

NAME AND NUMBER COMPARISONS

COMMENTARY

This test seeks to measure your ability and disposition to do a job carefully and accurately, your attention to exactness and preciseness of detail, your alertness and versatility in discerning similarities and differences between things, and your power in systematically handling written language symbols.

It is actually a test of your ability to do academic and/or clerical work, using the basic elements of verbal (qualitative) and mathematical (quantitative) learning—words and numbers.

EXAMINATION SECTION

TEST 1

DIRECTIONS: Questions 1 through 6 consist of sets of names and addresses. In each question, the name and address in Column II should be an exact copy of the name and address in Column II. *PRINT IN THE SPACE AT THE RIGHT THE LETTER*
- A. if there is a mistake only in the name
- B. if there is a mistake only in the address
- C. if there is a mistake in both name and address
- D. If there is no mistake in either name or address

SAMPLE:
Michael Filbert   Michael Filbert
456 Reade Street   644 Reade Street
New York, N.Y. 10013 New York, N.Y. 10013

Since there is a mistake only in the address, the answer is B.

1. Esta Wong   Esta Wang   1.____
   141 West 68 St.   141 West 68 St.
   New York, N.Y. 10023   New York, N.Y. 10023

2. Dr. Alberto Grosso   Dr. Alberto Grosso   2.____
   3475 12th Avenue   3475 12th Avenue
   Brooklyn, N.Y. 11218   Brooklyn, N.Y. 11218

3. Mrs. Ruth Bortlas   Ms. Ruth Bortias   3.____
   482 Theresa Ct.   482 Theresa Ct.
   Far Rockaway, N.Y. 11691   Far Rockaway, N.Y. 11169

4. Mr. and Mrs. Howard Fox   Mr. and Mrs. Howard Fox   4.____
   2301 Sedgwick Ave.   231 Sedgwick Ave.
   Bronx, N.Y. 10468   Bronx, N.Y. 10468

5. Miss Marjorie Black   Miss Margorie Black   5.____
   223 East 23 Street   223 East 23 Street
   New York, N.Y. 10010   New York, N.Y. 10010

2 (#1)

6. Michelle Herman Michelle Hermann 6._____
   806 Valley Rd. 806 Valley Dr.
   Old Tappan, N.J. 07675 Old Tappan, N.J. 07675

KEY (CORRECT ANSWERS)

1. A
2. D
3. C
4. B
5. A
6. C

TEST 2

DIRECTIONS: Questions 1 through 6 consist of sets of names and addresses. In each question, the name and address in Column II should be an exact copy of the name and address in Column II. *PRINT IN THE SPACE AT THE RIGHT THE LETTER*
- A. if there is a mistake only in the name
- B. if there is a mistake only in the address
- C. if there is a mistake in both name and address
- D. If there is no mistake in either name or address

#	Column I	Column II	Answer
1.	Ms. Joan Kelly 313 Franklin Ave. Brooklyn, N.Y. 11202	Ms. Joan Kielly 318 Franklin Ave. Brooklyn, N.Y. 11202	1.____
2.	Mrs. Eileen Engel 47-24 86 Road Queens, N.Y. 11122	Mrs. Ellen Engel 47-24 86 Road Queens, N.Y. 11122	2.____
3.	Marcia Michaels 213 E. 81 St. New York, N.Y. 10012	Marcia Michaels 213 E. 81 St. New York, N.Y. 10012	3.____
4.	Rev. Edward J. Smyth 1401 Brandeis Street San Francisco, Calif. 96201	Rev. Edward J. Smyth 1401 Brandies Street San Francisco, Calif. 96201	4.____
5.	Alicia Rodriguez 24-68 81 St. Elmhurst, N.Y. 11122	Alicia Rodriquez 2468 81 St. Elmhurst, N.Y. 11122	5.____
6.	Ernest Eissemann 21 Columbia St. New York, N.Y. 10007	Ernest Eisermann 21 Columbia St. New York, N.Y. 10007	6.____

KEY (CORRECT ANSWERS)

1. C
2. A
3. D
4. B
5. C
6. A

TEST 3

DIRECTIONS: Questions 1 through 8 consist of names, locations, and telephone numbers. In each question, the name, location and number in Column II should be an exact copy of the name, location, and number in Column I. *PRINT IN THE SPACE AT THE RIGHT THE LETTER*
- A. if there is a mistake in one line only
- B. if there is a mistake in two lines only
- C. if there is a mistake in three lines only
- D. if there are no mistakes in any of the lines

1. Ruth Lang
   EAM Bldg., Room C101
   625-2000, ext. 765

   Ruth Lang
   EAM Bldg., Room C110
   625-2000, ext. 765

   1._____

2. Anne Marie Ionozzi
   Investigations, Room 827
   576-4000, ext. 832

   Anna Marie Ionozzi
   Investigation, Room 827
   566-4000, ext. 832

   2._____

3. Willard Jameson
   Fm C Bldg. Room 687
   454-3010

   Willard Jamieson
   Fm C Bldg. Room 687
   454-3010

   3._____

4. Joanne Zimmermann
   Bldg. SW, Room 314
   532-4601

   Joanne Zimmermann
   Bldg. SW, Room 314
   532-4601

   4._____

5. Carlyle Whetstone
   Payroll Division-A, Room 212A
   262-5000, ext. 471

   Caryle Whetstone
   Payroll Division-A, Room 212A
   262-5000, ext. 417

   5._____

6. Kenneth Chiang
   Legal Council, Room 9745
   (201) 416-9100, ext. 17

   Kenneth Chiang
   Legal Counsel, Room 9745
   (201) 416-9100, ext. 17

   6._____

7. Ethel Koenig
   Personnel Services Div, Rm 433
   635-7572

   Ethel Hoenig
   Personal Services Div, Rm 433
   635-7527

   7._____

8. Joyce Ehrhardt
   Office of Administrator, Rm W56
   387-8706

   Joyce Ehrhart
   Office of Administrator, Rm W56
   387-7806

   8._____

2 (#3)

KEY (CORRECT ANSWERS)

1. A 6. A
2. C 7. C
3. A 8. B
4. D
5. B

TEST 4

DIRECTIONS: Each of Questions 1 through 10 gives the identification number and name of a person who has received treatment at a certain hospital. You are to choose the option (A, B, C, or D) which has EXACTLY the same number and name as those given in the question.

SAMPLE QUESTION:
123765 Frank Y. Jones
  A. 123675 Frank Y. Jones
  B. 123765 Frank T. Jones
  C. 123765 Frank Y. Jones
  D. 123765 Frank Y. Jones

The correct answer is D, because it is the only option showing the identification number and name exactly as they are in the sample question.

1. 754898 Diane Malloy
  A. 745898 Diane Malloy   B. 754898 Dion Malloy
  C. 754898 Diane Malloy   D. 754898 Diane Maloy

1.____

2. 661818 Ferdinand Figueroa
  A. 661818 Ferdinand Figeuroa   B. 661618 Ferdinand Figueroa
  C. 661818 Ferdnand Figueroa   D. 661818 Ferdinand Figueroa

2.____

3. 100101 Norman D. Braustein
  A. 100101 Norman D. Braustein   B. 101001 Norman D. Braustein
  C. 100101 Norman P. Braustien   D. 100101 Norman D. Bruastein

3.____

4. 838696 Robert Kittredge
  A. 838969 Robert Kittredge   B. 838696 Robert Kittredge
  C. 388696 Robert Kittredge   D. 838696 Robert Kittridge

4.____

5. 243716 Abraham Soletsky
  A. 243716 Abrahm Soletsky   B. 243716 Abraham Solestky
  C. 243176 Abraham Soletsky   D. 243716 Abraham Soletsky

5.____

6. 981121 Phillip M. Maas
  A. 981121 Phillip M. Mass   B. 981211 Phillip M. Maas
  C. 981121 Phillip M. Maas   D. 981121 Phillip N. Maas

6.____

7. 786556 George Macalusso
  A. 785656 George Macalusso   B. 786556 George Macalusso
  C. 786556 George Maculusso   D. 786556 George Macluasso

7.____

8. 639472 Eugene Weber
  A. 639472 Eugene Weber   B. 639472 Eugene Webre
  C. 693472 Eugene Weber   D. 639742 Eugene Weber

8.____

2 (#4)

9. 724936 John J. Lomonaco 9._____
   A. 724936 John J. Lomanoco B. 724396 John L. Lomonaco
   C. 7224936 John J. Lomonaco D. 724936 John J. Lamonaco

10. 899868 Michael Schnitzer 10._____
    A. 899868 Micheal Schnitzer B. 898968 Michael Schnizter
    C. 899688 Michael Schnitzer D. 899868 Michael Schnitzer

KEY (CORRECT ANSWERS)

1.	C	6.	C
2.	D	7.	B
3.	A	8.	A
4.	B	9.	C
5.	D	10.	D

FILING
EXAMINATION SECTION
TEST 1

Questions 1-9.

DIRECTIONS: An important part of the duties of an office worker in a public agency is to file office records. Questions 1 through 9 are designed to determine whether you can file records correctly. Each of these questions consists of four names. For each question, select the one of the four names that should be FOURTH if the four names were arranged in alphabetical order. *PRINT THE LETTER OF THE CORRECT ANSWER IN THE SPACE AT THE RIGHT.*

1. A. 6th National Bank
   C. The 69th Street League
   B. Sexton Lock Co.
   D. Thomas Saxon Corp.
   1.____

2. A. 4th Avenue Printing Co.
   C. Dr. Milton Fournet
   B. The Four Corners Corp.
   D. The Martin Fountaine Co.
   2.____

3. A. Mr. Chas. Le Mond
   C. Lenox Enterprises
   B. Model Express, Inc.
   D. Mobile Supply Co.
   3.____

4. A. Frank Waller Johnson
   C. Wilson Johnson
   B. Frank Walter Johnson
   D. Frank W. Johnson
   4.____

5. A. Miss Anne M. Carlsen
   C. Mr. Alan Ross Carlsen
   B. Mrs. Albert S. Carlson
   D. Dr. Anthony Ash Carlson
   5.____

6. A. Delaware Paper Co.
   C. Ralph A. Delmar
   B. William Del Ville
   D. Wm. K. Del Ville
   6.____

7. A. The Lloyd Disney Co.
   C. Oklahoma Envelope, Inc.
   B. Mrs. Raymond Norris
   D. Miss Esther O'Neill
   7.____

8. A. The Olympic Eraser Co.
   C. Oklahoma Envelope, Inc.
   B. Mrs. Raymond Norris
   D. Miss Esther O'Neill
   8.____

9. A. Patricia MacNamara
   C. Robt. MacPherson, Jr.
   B. Eleanor McNally
   D. Helen McNair
   9.____

Questions 10-21.

DIRECTIONS: Questions 10 through 21 are to be answered on the basis of the usual rules for alphabetical filing. For each question, indicate in the space at the right the letter preceding the name which should be THIRD in alphabetical order.

10. A. Russell Cohen   B. Henry Cohn   10.____
    C. Wesley Chambers   D. Arthur Connors

11. A. Wanda Jenkins   B. Pauline Jennings   11.____
    C. Leslie Jantzenberg D. Rudy Jensen

12. A. Arnold Wilson   B. Carlton Willson   12.____
    C. Duncan Williamson D. Ezra Wilston

13. A. Joseph M. Buchman B. Gustave Bozzerman   13.____
    C. Constantino Brunelli D. Armando Buccino

14. A. Barbara Waverly   B. Corinne Warterdam   14.____
    C. Dennis Waterman   D. Harold Wartman

15. A. Jose Mejia   B. Bernard Mendelsohn 15.____
    C. Antonio Mejias   D. Richard Mazzitelli

16. A. Hesselberg, Norman J. B. Hesselman, Nathan B. 16.____
    C. Hazel, Robert S. D. Heintz, August J.

17. A. Oshins, Jerome   B. Ohsie, Marjorie   17.____
    C. O'Shaugn, F.J.   D. O'Shea, Frances

18. A. Petrie, Joshua A. B. Pendleton, Oscar   18.____
    C. Pertwee, Joshua   D. Perkins, Warren G.

19. A. Morganstern, Alfred B. Morganstern, Albert 19.____
    C. Monroe, Mildred   D. Modesti, Ernest

20. A. More, Stewart   B. Moorhead, Jay   20.____
    C. Moore, Benjamin   D. Moffat, Edith

21. A. Ramirez, Paul   B. Revere, Pauline   21.____
    C. Ramos, Felix   D. Ramazotti, Angelo

KEY (CORRECT ANSWERS)

1.	C		11.	B
2.	A		12.	A
3.	B		13.	D
4.	B		14.	C
5.	D		15.	C
6.	A		16.	A
7.	C		17.	D
8.	D		18.	C
9.	B		19.	B
10.	B		20.	B

21. C

TEST 2

DIRECTIONS: Each question or incomplete statement is followed by several suggested answers or completions. Select the one that BEST answers the question or completes the statement. *PRINT THE LETTER OF THE CORRECT ANSWER IN THE SPACE AT THE RIGHT.*

Questions 1-4.

DIRECTIONS: Questions 1 through 4 are to be answered on the basis of the following alphabetical rules.

RULES FOR ALPHABETICAL FILING

Names of Individuals

The names of individuals are filed in strict alphabetical order, *first* according to the last name, *then* according to first name or initial, and *finally* according to middle name or initial. For example: George Allen precedes Edward Bell and Leonard Reston precedes Lucille Reston.

When last names are the same, for example, A. Green and Agnes Green, the one with the initial comes before the one with the name written out when the first initials are identical.

Prefixes such as De, O', Mac, Mc and Van are filed as written and are treated as part of the names to which they are connected. For example, Gladys McTeaque is filed before Frances Meadows.

1. If the following four names were put into an alphabetical list, what would the FIRST name on the list be?
    A. Wm. C. Paul
    B. W. Paul
    C. Alice Paul
    D. Alyce Paule

2. If the following four names were put into an alphabetical list, what would the THIRD name on the list be?
    A. I. MacCarthy
    B. Irene MacKarthy
    C. Ida McCaren
    D. I.A. McCarthy

3. If the following four names were put into an alphabetical list, what would the SECOND name on the list be?
    A. John Gilhooley
    B. Ramon Gonzalez
    C. Gerald Gilholy
    D. Samuel Gilvecchio

4. If the following four names were put into an alphabetical list, what would the FOURTH name on the list be?
    A. Michael Edwinn
    B. James Edwards
    C. Mary Edwin
    D. Carlo Edwards

Questions 5-9.

DIRECTIONS: Questions 5 through 9 consist of a group of names which are to be arranged in alphabetical order for filing.

5. Of the following, the name which should be filed FIRST is
   A. Joseph J. Meadeen
   B. Gerard L. Meader
   C. John F. Madcar
   D. Philip F. Malder

6. Of the following, the name which should be filed LAST is
   A. Stephen Fischer
   B. Benjamin Fitchmann
   C. Thomas Fishman
   D. Augustus S. Fisher

7. The name which should be filed SECOND is
   A. Yeatman, Frances
   B. Yeaton, C.S.
   C. Yeatman, R.M.
   D. Yeats, John

8. The name which should be filed THIRD is
   A. Hauser, Ann
   B. Hauptmann, Jane
   C. Hauster, Mary
   D. Rauprich, Julia

9. The name which should be filed SECOND is
   A. Flora McDougall
   B. Fred E. MacDowell
   C. Juanita Mendez
   D. James A. Madden

Questions 10-14.

DIRECTIONS: Questions 10 through 14 are to be answered based on an alphabetical arrangement of the following list of names.

Walker, Carol J.	Wacht, Michael	Wade, Ethel
Wall, Fredrick	Wall, Francis	Wall, Frank
Wachs, Paul	Walker, Carol L.	Wagner, Arthur
Walters, Daniel	Wade, Ellen	Wald, William
Wagner, Allen	Walters, David	Walker, Carmen

10. The 4th name on the alphabetized list would be
    A. Wade, Ellen
    B. Wade, Ethel
    C. Wagner, Allen
    D. Wagner, Arthur

11. The 7th name on the alphabetized list would be
    A. Walker, Carmen
    B. Walker, Carol J.
    C. Walker, Carol L.
    D. Wald, William

12. The name that would come immediately AFTER Wagner, Arthur on the alphabetized list would be
    A. Wade, Ethel
    B. Wagner, Allen
    C. Wald, William
    D. Walker, Carol L.

13. The name that would come immediately BEFORE Wall, Frank would be   13._____
    A. Wall, Francis   B. Wall, Fredrick
    C. Walters, David   D. Walters, Daniel

14. The 12th name on the alphabetized list would be   14._____
    A. Walker, Carol L.   B. Wald, William
    C. Wall, Francis   D. Wall, Frank

KEY (CORRECT ANSWERS)

1. C	6. B	11. D
2. C	7. C	12. C
3. A	8. A	13. A
4. A	9. D	14. D
5. C	10. B	

TEST 3

DIRECTIONS: Each question or incomplete statement is followed by several suggested answers or completions. Select the one that BEST answers the question or completes the statement. *PRINT THE LETTER OF THE CORRECT ANSWER IN THE SPACE AT THE RIGHT.*

Questions 1-8.

DIRECTIONS: Questions 1 through 8 are based on the Rules of Alphabetical Filing given below. Read these rules carefully before answering the questions.

Names of People

1. The names of people are filed in strict alphabetical order, first according to the last name, then according to first name or initial, and finally according to middle name or initial. For example: George Allen comes before Edward Bell, and Leonard P. Reston comes before Lucille B. Reston.

2. When last names are the same, for example, A. Green and Agnes Green, the one with the initial comes before the one with the name written out when the first initials are identical.

3. When first and last names are alike and the middle name is given, for example, John David Doe and John Devoe Doe, the names should be filed in alphabetical order of the middle names.

4. When first and last names are the same, a name without a middle initial comes before one with a middle name or initial. For example, John Doe comes before John A. Doe and John Alan Doe.

5. When first and last names are the same, a name with a middle initial comes before one with a middle name beginning with the same initial. For example, Jack R. Hertz comes before Jack Richard Hertz.

6. Prefixes such as De, O', Mac, Mc, and Van are filed as written and are treated as part of the names to which they are connected. For example, Robert O'Dea is filed before David Olsen.

7. Abbreviated names are treated as if they were spelled out. For example: Chas. is filed as Charles and Thos. is filed as Thomas.

8. Titles and designations such as Dr., Mr., and Prof. are disregarded in filing.

Names of Organizations

1. The names of business organizations are filed according to the order in which each word in the name appears. When an organization name bears the name of a person, it is filed according to the rules for filing names of people as given above. For example: William Smith Service Co. comes before Television Distributors, Inc.

2. Where bureau, board, office or department appears as the first part of the title of a governmental agency, that agency should be filed under the word in the title expressing the chief function of the agency. For example, Bureau of Budget would be filed as if written Budget, (Bureau of the). The Department of Personnel would be filed as if written Personnel, (Department of).

3. When the following words are part of an organization, they are disregarded: the, of, and.

4. When there are numbers in a name, they are treated as if they were spelled out. For example: 10th Street Bootery is filed as Tenth Street Bootery.

Each question from 1 through 8 contains four names numbered from 1 through 4 but not necessarily numbered in correct filing order. Answer each question by choosing the letter corresponding to the CORRECT filing order of the four names in accordance with the above rules.

SAMPLE QUESTION:
 I. Robert J. Smith
 II. R. Jeffrey Smith
 III. Dr. A. Smythe
 IV. Allen R. Smithers

A. I, II, III, IV   B. III, I, II, IV   C. II, I, IV, III   D. III, II, I, IV

Since the correct filing order, in accordance with the above rules is II I, IV, III, the correct answer is C.

1. I. J. Chester VanClief   II. John C. Van Clief
   III. J. VanCleve   IV. Mary L. Vance

   The CORRECT answer is:
   A. IV, III, I, II   B. IV, III, II, I   C. III, I, II, IV   D. III, IV, I, II

2. I. Community Development Agency   II. Department of Social Services
   III. Board of Estimate   IV. Bureau of Gas and Electricity

   The CORRECT answer is:
   A. III, IV, I, II   B. 1, II, IV, III   C. II, I, III, IV   D. I, III, IV, II

3. I. Dr. Chas. K. Dahlman   II. F. & A. Delivery Service
   III. Department of Water Supply   IV. Demano Men's Custom Tailors

   The CORRECT answer is:
   A. I, II, III, IV   B. I, IV, II, III   C. IV, I, II, III   D. IV, I, III, II

2 (#3)

4. I. 48th Street Theater II. Fourteenth Street Day Care Center 4.____
    III. Professor A. Cartwright IV. Albert F. McCarthy

    The CORRECT answer is:
    A. IV, II, I, III   B. IV, III, I, II   C. III, II, I, IV   D. III, I, II, IV

5. I. Frances D'Arcy II. Mario L. DelAmato 5.____
    III. William R. Diamond IV. Robert J. DuBarry

    The CORRECT answer is:
    A. I, II, IV, III   B. II, I, III, IV   C. I, II, III, IV   D. II, I, III, IV

6. I. Evelyn H. D'Amelio II. Jane R. Bailey 6.____
    III. Robert Bailey IV. Frank Baily

    The CORRECT answer is:
    A. I, II, III, IV   B. I, III, II, IV   C. II, III, IV, I   D. III, II, IV, I

7. I. Department of Markets 7.____
    II. Bureau of Handicapped Children
    III. Housing Authority Administration Building
    IV. Board of Pharmacy

    The CORRECT answer is:
    A. II, I, III, IV   B. I, II, IV, III   C. I, II, III, IV   D. III, II, I, IV

8. I. William A. Shea Stadium II. Rapid Speed Taxi Co. 8.____
    III. Harry Stampler's Rotisserie III. Wilhelm Albert Shea

    The CORRECT answer is:
    A. II, III, IV, I   B. IV, I, III, II   C. II, IV, I, III   D. III, IV, I, II

Questions 9-18.

DIRECTIONS: Questions 9 through 18 each show in Column I names written on four ledger cards (lettered w, x, y, z) which have to be filed. You are to choose the option (lettered A, B, C, or D) in Column II which BEST represents the proper order for filing the cards.

SAMPLE

COLUMN I | COLUMN II
w. John Stevens | A. w, y, z, x
x. John D. Stevenson | B. y, w, z, x
y. Joan Stevens | C. x, y, w, z
z. J. Stevenson | D. x, w, y, z

141

3 (#3)

The correct way to file the cards is:
y. Joan Stevens
w. John Stevens
z. J. Stevenson
x. John D. Stevenson

The correct order is shown by the letters y, w, z, x in that sequence. Since, in Column II, B appears in front of the letters y, w, z, x in that sequence, B is the correct answer to the sample question.

Now answer the following questions, using the same procedure.

9. COLUMN I
    w. Juan Montoya
    x. Manuel Montenegro
    y. Victor Matos
    z. Victoria Maltos

    COLUMN II
    A. y, z, x, w
    B. z, y, x, w
    C. z, y, w, x
    D. y, x, z, w

    9.____

10. COLUMN I
    w. Frank Carlson
    x. Robert Carlson
    y. George Carlson
    z. Frank Carlton

    COLUMN II
    A. z, x, w, y
    B. z, y, x, w
    C. w, y, z, x
    D. w, z, y, x

    10.____

11. COLUMN I
    w. Carmine Rivera
    x. Jose Rivera
    y. Frank River
    z. Joan Rivers

    COLUMN II
    A. y, w, x, z
    B. y, x, w, z
    C. w, x, y, z
    D. w, x, z, y

    11.____

12. COLUMN I
    w. Jerome Mathews
    x. Scott A. Matthew
    y. Charles B. Matthew
    z. Scott C. Mathewsw

    COLUMN II
    A. w, y, z, x
    B. z, y, x, w
    C. z, w, x, y
    D. w, z, y, x

    12.____

13. COLUMN I
    w. John McMahan
    x. John P. MacMahan
    y. Joseph DeMayo
    z. Joseph D. Mayo

    COLUMN II
    A. w, x, y, z
    B. y, x, z, w
    C. x, w, y, z
    D. y, x, w, z

    13.____

14. COLUMN I
    w. Raymond Martinez
    x. Ramon Martinez
    y. Prof. Ray Martinez
    z. Dr. Raymond Martin

    COLUMN II
    A. z, x, y, w
    B. z, y, x, w
    C. z, w, y, x
    D. y, x, w, z

    14.____

4 (#3)

15. COLUMN I
　w. Mr. Robert Vincent Mackintosh
　x. Robert Reginald Macintosh
　y. Roger V. McIntosh
　z. Robert R. Mackintosh

　COLUMN II
　A. y, x, z, w
　B. x, w, z, y
　C. x, w, y, z
　D. x, z, w, y

15.____

16. COLUMN I
　w. Dr. D. V. Facsone
　x. Prof. David Fascone
　y. Donald Facsone
　z. Mrs. D. Fascone

　COLUMN II
　A. y, w, z, x
　B. w, y, x, z
　C. w, y, z, x
　D. z, w, x, y

16.____

17. COLUMN I
　w. Johnathan Q. Addams
　x. John Quincy Adams
　y. J. Quincy Addams
　z. Jerimiah Adams

　COLUMN II
　A. z, x, w, y
　B. z, x, y, w
　C. y, w, x, z
　D. x, w, z, y

17.____

18. COLUMN I
　w. Nehimiah Persoff
　x. Newton Pershing
　y. Newman Perring
　z. Nelson Persons

　COLUMN II
　A. w, z, x, y
　B. x, z, y, w
　C. y, x, w, z
　D. z, y, w, x

18.____

KEY (CORRECT ANSWERS)

1. A	6. D	11. A	16. C
2. D	7. D	12. D	17. B
3. B	8. C	13. B	18. C
4. D	9. B	14. A	
5. C	10. C	15. D	

TEST 4

Questions 1-13.

DIRECTIONS: Each question from 1 through 13 contains four names. For each question, choose the name that should be FIRST if he four names are to be arranged in alphabetical order in accordance with the Rule for Alphabetical Filing of Names of People given below. Read this rule carefully. Then, for each question, mark your answer space with the letter that is next to the name that should be first in alphabetical order.

RULE FOR ALPHABETICAL FILING OF NAMES OF PEOPLE

The names of people are filed in strict alphabetical order, first according to the last name, then according to the first name. For example; George Allen comes before Edward Bell, and Alice Reston comes before Lucille Reston.

SAMPLE QUESTION
A. Roger Smith (2)
B. Joan Smythe (4)
C. Alan Smith (1)
D. James Smithe (3)

The number in parentheses show the proper alphabetical order in which these names should be filed. Since the name that should be filed FIRST is Alan Smith, the correct answer to the sample question is C.

1. A. William Claremont   B. Antonio Clements
   C. Anthony Clemente   D. William Claymont   1._____

2. A. Wayne Fumando   B. Sarah Femando
   C. Susan Fumando   D. Wilson Femando   2._____

3. A. Wilbur Hanson   B. Wm. Hansen
   C. Robert Hansen   D. Thomas Hanson   3._____

4. A. George St. John   B. Thomas Santos
   C. Frances Starks   D. Mary S. Stranum   4._____

5. A. Franklin Carrol   B. Timothy Carrol
   C. Timothy S. Carol   D. Frank F. Carroll   5._____

6. A. Christie-Barry Storage   B. John Christie-Barry
   C. The Christie-Barry Company   D. Anne Christie-Barrie   6._____

7. A. Inter State Travel Co.   A. Interstate Car Rental
   C. Inter State Trucking   D. Interstate Lending Inst.   7._____

144

2 (#4)

8. A. The Los Angeles Tile Co. 8.____
    B. Anita F. Los
    C. The Lost & Found Detective Agency
    D. Jason Los-Brio

9. A. Prince Charles   B. Prince Charles Coiffures   9.____
    C. Chas. F. Prince   D. Thomas A. Charles

10. A. U.S. Dept. of Agriculture   B. United States Aircraft Co.   10.____
    C. U.S. Air Transport, Inc.   D. The United Union

11. A. Meyer's Art Shop   B. Frank B. Meyer   11.____
    C. Meyers' Paint Store   D. Meyer and Goldberg

12. A. David Des Laurier   B. Des Moines Flower Shop   12.____
    C. Henry Desanto   D. Mary L. Desta

13. A. Jeffrey Van Der Meer   B. Jeffrey M. Vander   13.____
    C. Jeffrey Van   D. Wallace Meer

KEY (CORRECT ANSWERS)

1.	A	6.	D	11.	A
2.	B	7.	B	12.	C
3.	C	8.	B	13.	D
4.	A	9.	D		
5.	C	10.	C		

TEST 5

Questions 1-10.

DIRECTIONS: Questions 1 through 10 are to be answered on the basis of the usual rules of filing. Column I lists, next to the numbers 1 to 10, the names of 10 clinic patients. Column II lists, next to the letters A to D, the headings of file drawers into which you are to place the records of these patients. For each question, indicate in the space at the right the letter preceding the heading of the file drawer in which the record should be filed.

COLUMN I	COLUMN II	
1. Charles Coughlin	A. Cab-Cep	1.____
2. Mary Carstairs	B. Ceq-Cho	2.____
3. Joseph Collin	C. Chr-Coj	3.____
4. Thomas Chelsey	D. Cok-Czy	4.____
5. Cedric Chalmers		5.____
6. Mae Clarke		6.____
7. Dora Copperhead		7.____
8. Arnold Cohn		8.____
9. Charlotte Crumboldt		9.____
10. Frances Celine		10.____

Questions 11-18.

DIRECTIONS: Questions 11 to 18 are to be answered on the basis of the usual rules of filing. Column I lists, next to the numbers 11 to 18, the names of 8 clinic patients. Column II lists, next to the letters A to O, the headings of file drawers into which you are to place the records of these patients. For each question, indicate in the space at the right the letter preceding the heading of the file drawer in which the record should be filed.

2 (#5)

	COLUMN I	COLUMN II	
11.	Thomas Adams	A. Aab-Abi	11._____
		B. Abj-Ach	
12.	Joseph Albert	C. Aci-Aco	12._____
		D. Acp-Ada	
13.	Frank Anaster	E. Adb-Afr	13._____
		F. Afs-Ago	
14.	Charles Abt	G. Agp-Ahz	14._____
		H. Aia-Ako	
15.	John Alfred	I. Akp-Ald	15._____
		J. Ale-Amo	
16.	Louis Aron	K. Amp-Aor	16._____
		L. Aos-Apr	
17.	Francis Amos	M. Aps-Asi	17._____
		N. Asj-Ati	
18.	William Adler	O. Atj-Awz	18._____

Questions 19-28.

DIRECTIONS: Questions 19 through 28 are to be answered on the basis of the usual rules of filing. Column I lists, next to the numbers 19 through 28, the names of 10 clinic patients. Column II lists, next to the letters A to D the headings of file drawers into which you are to place the medical records of these patients. For each question, indicate in the space at the right the letter preceding the heading of the file drawer in which the record should be filed.

	COLUMN I	COLUMN II	
19.	Frank Shea	A. Sab-Sej	19._____
20.	Rose Seaborn	B. Sek-Sio	20._____
21.	Samuel Smollin	C. Sip-Soo	21._____
22.	Thomas Shur	D. Sop-Syz	22._____
23.	Ben Schaefer		23._____
24.	Shirley Strauss		24._____
25.	Harry Spiro		25._____
26.	Dora Skelly		26._____
27.	Sylvia Smith		27._____
28.	Arnold Selz		28._____

KEY (CORRECT ANSWERS)

1.	D	11.	D	21.	C
2.	A	12.	I	22.	B
3.	D	13.	K	23.	A
4.	B	14.	B	24.	D
5.	B	15.	J	25.	D
6.	C	16.	M	26.	C
7.	D	17.	J	27.	C
8.	C	18.	E	28.	B
9.	D	19.	B		
10.	A	20.	A		

BASIC NURSING PROCEDURES: TAKING TEMPERATURE, PULSE, AND BLOOD PRESSURE

CONTENTS

		Page
I.	TAKING ORAL TEMPERATURE	
	A. Thermometers Disinfected on Ward	1
	B. Individual Thermometer Technique	4
	C. Taking Temperatures With the Electronic Thermometer	6
II.	TAKING AXILLARY TEMPERATURE	7
III.	TAKING RECTAL TEMPERATURE	8
	A. Thermometers Disinfected on Ward	8
	B. Thermometers Disinfected in Central Supply Room	9
IV.	TAKING PULSE AND RESPIRATION	10
V.	APICAL-RADIAL PULSE	11
VI.	TAKING BLOOD PRESSURE	12
VII.	RECORDING ON THE TEMPERATURE, PULSE, AND RESPIRATION FORM	13
VIII.	RECORDING ON PLOTTING CHART	19

BASIC NURSING PROCEDURES: TAKING TEMPERATURE, PULSE, AND BLOOD PRESSURE

I. TAKING ORAL TEMPERATURE
A. THERMOMETERS DISINFECTED ON WARD

PURPOSE

To determine the patient's body temperature as recorded on a clinical thermometer.

EQUIPMENT
1. Tray containing:
    a. Two containers of disinfecting agent marked #1 and #2
    b. Container of green soap solution
    c. Container of water
    d. Container of clean cotton
    e. Waste container for soiled cotton
    f. Minimum of 6 thermometers, 3 in each container of disinfecting solution
    g. T.P.R. book
    h. Pencil and pen
    i. Watch with second hand

PROCEDURE
1. Take equipment to bedside.
2. Tell the patient what you are going to do.
3. Remove thermometer from container #1.
4. Wipe thermometer (over waste container) with water moistened sponge from stem to bulb using rotary motion. Discard sponge in waste container.
5. Shake down thermometer mercury to 95° F.
6. Place thermometer under patient's tongue. Caution him to keep his lips closed.
7. Distribute other thermometers to second and third patients in same manner.
8. Take third patient's pulse and respiration. Record results in T.P.R. book.
9. Take pulse and respiration of second patient, record, then first patient. Record results in T.P.R. book.
10. Remove thermometer from first patient's mouth after 3 minutes.
11. Wash thermometer (over waste container) with soap-moistened sponge from stem to bulb using rotary motion. Discard sponge in waste container.

PROCEDURE (Continued)

12. Moisten cotton sponge with water and wipe thermometer from stem to bulb in a rotary container. Discard sponge in waste container.
13. Read thermometer. Record results in T.P.R. book.
14. Place thermometer in the _original_ container of disinfecting agent.
15. Repeat the steps 10 through 13 for second and third patients.
16. Disinfect these thermometers for a minimum of 20 minutes (depending on disinfecting agent used).
17. Continue using thermometers from alternate containers until all patient's temperatures have been taken.
18. Record T.P.R.'s on SP 511.

CARE OF EQUIPMENT

1. After each use
    a. Remove waste.
    b. Clean tray.
    c. Reset tray.
    d. Replace solutions (water - soap).
2. Daily
    a. Wash containers in warm, soapy water, rinse and dry.
    b. Change all solutions.
    c. Wash thermometers in cold, soapy water, rinse and place in disinfecting agent.
    d. Refill and reset tray.

POINTS TO EMPHASIZE

1. Wait for 10 minutes before taking temperature of patient who has had hot or cold drink or who has been smoking.
2. Be sure thermometer reads 95 or below before using it.
3. Encircle abnormal vital signs with red pencil in T.P.R. book.
4. Report all abnormal vital signs to Charge Nurse.
5. Describe quality of pulse and respiration in the observation column on Nursing Notes (SF 510).

POINTS TO EMPHASIZE (Continued)

6. After washing thermometer with soap, be sure to rinse well with water before putting it into disinfectant, as bacterial action is nullified in the presence of soap; for example, Zephiran chloride and iodine preparations.
7. Individual thermometers should be used for patients suspected of having a communicable disease.

THERMOMETERS STERILIZED IN CENTRAL SUPPLY ROOM

EQUIPMENT

1. Tray containing:
    a. Container of sterile oral thermometers that are sealed in paper envelopes.
    b. Container of green soap solution.
    c. Container of clean cotton.
    d. Container for waste material.
    e. T.P.R. book.
    f. Pencil.
    g. Watch with second hand.

PROCEDURE

1. Tell the patient what you are going to do.
2. Remove thermometer from envelope.
3. Shake thermometer mercury to 95° F.
4. Place thermometer under patient's tongue. Caution him to keep his lips closed.
5. Take, record and report vital signs as in previous procedure, numbers 7 through 11, pages 25 and 26.

CARE OF EQUIPMENT

1. After each use:
    a. Empty container of waste cotton.
    b. Return container of soiled thermometers to CSR in accordance with local instructions and exchange for an adequate supply of clean thermometers.
    c. Reset tray.
2. Daily:
    a. Wash containers in warm, soapy water, rinse and dry.
    b. Refill and reset tray.

TAKING ORAL TEMPERATURE
B. INDIVIDUAL THERMOMETER TECHNIQUE

PURPOSE

To determine the patient's body temperature as recorded on a clinical thermometer.

EQUIPMENT

1. Individual thermometer for each patient at bedside
2. Plastic thermometer holder with disinfectant solution - protective container of 2 1/2 cc. disposable syringe can be used
3. Adhesive tape
4. Container of clean cotton balls
5. Container for soiled cotton balls
6. T.P.R. book and pen
7. Watch with second hand

PROCEDURE

1. Upon admission, set up thermometer and holder at patient's unit:
   a. Fill thermometer holder (protective container from a 2 1/2 cc. disposable syringe) with disinfectant.
   b. Place thermometer inside container.
   c. Tape container to head of bed or side of bedside locker.
2. When taking temperatures:
   a. Take containers for cotton balls to bedside.
   b. Tell patient what you are going to do.
   c. Remove thermometer from holder.
   d. Wipe thermometer with clean cotton ball. Discard cotton ball in waste container.
   e. Shake down thermometer mercury to 95° F.
   f. Place thermometer under patient's tongue.
   g. Follow above steps to second and third patient,
   h. Take third patient's pulse and respiration. Record results in T.P.R. book.
   i. Take pulse and respiration of second patient, record, then first patient,
   j. Remove thermometer from first patient's mouth after 3 minutes.
   k. Wipe thermometer with clean cotton ball. Discard cotton ball in waste container.
   l. Read thermometer and replace in holder. Record results in T.P.R. book,
   m. Repeat steps j through l for second and third patient.

CARE OF EQUIPMENT
1. After each use:
   a. Discard soiled cotton balls and container.
2. Weekly and when patient is discharged:
   a. Collect thermometers and holders.
   b. Disinfect thermometers as outlined on page 26.
   c. Place in new holders containing disinfectant.
   d. Discard old holders.
   e. Replace thermometers and holders at bedside.

C. TAKING TEMPERATURES WITH THE ELECTRONIC THERMOMETER

PURPOSE
To determine the patient's body temperature with an electronic thermometer which is a beat sending device with an accuracy of a plus or minus of .2 degrees. It utilizes a disposable probe cover and records oral and rectal temperatures within 15 seconds.

EQUIPMENT
1. Base for electronic thermometer
2. Thermometer with oral probe (sensing device)
3. Rectal probes where applicable
4. Disposable probe covers

PROCEDURE
1. Remove probe from base which is connected to electricity.
2. Attach strap of thermometer around shoulder to secure thermometer to side (left side if right handed).
3. Remove probe and insert probe into disposable probe cover.
4. Turn thermometer on by pressing small bar on top.
5. Place covered probe into patient's mouth in the sublingual area and slowly push probe along the base of the tongue as far back as possible without discomfort to the patient.
6. Hold probe in place until indicator on thermometer records a completed thermometer reading.
7. Transfer reading to appropriate records.
8. Eject the disposable probe cover.
9. Press bar on back of thermometer erasing present reading and repeat the above procedure for the next patient.
10. Remove thermometer pack and replace securely in base for recharging thermometer.

POINTS TO EMPHASIZE
1. Grasp probe at reinforced area in the center to decrease breakage.
2. Always keep base plugged into electrical current.
3. Always keep thermometer in base when not in use to keep the battery charged.
4. Use specified probe for rectal temperature and insert probe cover 1/2 inch on adults or 1/4 inch on babies for accurate recordings.
5. For axillary temperatures do not press bar to activate thermometer until the oral probe with cover is in place, then allow 60-90 seconds for recording of temperature. Indicator will not come on.

II. TAKING AXILLARY TEMPERATURE

PURPOSE

To determine a patient's temperature when the oral or rectal route is contraindicated.

EQUIPMENT

Oral thermometer tray
T.P.R. book
Pencil or pen
Watch with a second hand

PROCEDURE

Same as for oral temperature (pages 1 and 2) except:
1. Wipe axilla dry.
2. Place oral thermometer in axilla. Have patient cross arms over chest.
3. Leave thermometer in place for 10 minutes.
4. Write "A" above temperature in T.P.R. book, and T.P.R. graph (SF 511).

III. TAKING RECTAL TEMPERATURE
A. THERMOMETERS DISINFECTED ON WARD

PURPOSE

To determine patient's temperature when the oral method is contraindicated.

EQUIPMENT

1. Tray containing
   a. Two containers of disinfecting agent marked #1 and #2
   b. Container of green soap solution
   c. Container of water
   d. Container of clean cotton sponges
   e. Container for waste cotton sponges
   f. Minimum of 4 thermometers in container #1 of disinfecting agent. (Number of thermometers determined by ward needs).
   g. Tube of water soluble lubricant
   h. T.P.R. book
   i. Pencil and pen
   j. Watch with second hand

PROCEDURE

1. Take equipment to bedside.
2. Tell patient what you are going to do.
3. Remove thermometer from container fl.
4. Wipe thermometer (over waste container) with water moistened sponge from stem to bulb using a rotary motion. Discard sponge in waste container.
5. Shake thermometer mercury to 95° F.
6. Lubricate thermometer with water soluble lubricant.
7. Turn patient on side unless contraindicated.
8. Separate buttocks and gently insert thermometer 1 1/2 inches into the rectum in an upward and forward direction. Insert 1/2 - 3/4 inch in infants and children.
9. Hold thermometer in place for 5 minutes. Count pulse and respiration and record in T.P.R. book.
10. Remove thermometer.
11. Wash thermometer (over waste container) with soap moistened sponge from stem to bulb using rotary motion. Discard sponge in waste container.
12. Moisten cotton sponge with water and wipe thermometer from stem to bulb in a rotary motion. Discard sponge in waste container.
13. Read thermometer and record temperature in T.P.R. book. Place "R" above recording to indicate that it was taken rectally.
14. Return thermometer to glass #2 for sterilization for a minimum of 20 minutes.
15. Leave patient in comfortable position.

16. Record T.P.R.'s on SF 511. Use "R" to indicate rectal temperature.
17. Continue taking additional rectal temperatures in the same manner.

CARE OF EQUIPMENT
1. After each use
   a. Remove waste.
   b. Clean tray.
   c. Transfer thermometers from container 12 to container #1 after 20 minutes has elapsed.
   d. Replace water and soap solution.
   e. Reset tray.
2. Daily
   a. Wash containers in warm, soapy water, rinse and dry.
   b. Change all solutions.
   c. Wash thermometers in cold, soapy water, rinse well and place in disinfectant agent.
   d. Refill and reset tray.

POINTS TO EMPHASIZE
1. Wait 30 minutes before taking temperature on patient who has had an enema.
2. Use only a stub bulb thermometer expressly made for rectal use.
3. Do not leave patient unattended while thermometer is inserted.
4. Report abnormal vital signs to Charge Nurse.
5. Describe the quality of pulse and respirations in observation column on Nursing Notes (SF 510). On wards where many rectal temperatures are taken, (for example, Pediatrics, ICU, etc.), increase the number of thermometers in each container. Continue using thermometers from alternate containers, allowing at least 20 minutes for sterilization, until all patients' temperatures are taken.
6. Be sure to rinse thermometer well before putting it into the disinfectant, as bacterial action is nullified in the presence of soap - for example, Zephiran chloride and iodine preparations.

B. THERMOMETERS DISINFECTED IN CENTRAL SUPPLY ROOM

EQUIPMENT
1. Tray containing
   a. Container of rectal thermometers sealed in paper envelopes
   b. Container of clean cotton sponges
   c. Container of soap solution
   d. Container for waste cotton sponges
   e. Container for used thermometers
   f. Tube of water soluble lubricant

g. T.P.R. book
h. Pencil or pen
i. Watch with second hand

PROCEDURE
1. Remove thermometer from envelope.
2. Take, record and report vital signs as in previous procedure page 30.
3. Return thermometer to container of soap solution for return to C.S.R.

CARE OF EQUIPMENT
1. After each use
   Remove waste
   Clean tray
2. Daily
   Return container of thermometers to C.S.R. in accordance with local instructions and exchange for supply of sterile thermometers.
   Wash containers in warm/ soapy water, rinse and dry.
   Refill and reset tray.

IV. TAKING PULSE AND RESPIRATION

PURPOSE

To determine the character and rate of the pulse and respiration.

EQUIPMENT
Watch with a second hand
Pencil or pen
T. P. R. book

PROCEDURE
1. Tell patient what he is to do.
2. Have the patient lie down or sit in chair. Draw his arm and hand across his chest.
3. Place three fingers over the radial artery on the thumb side of the patient's wrist. Use just enough pressure to feel the pulse beat.
4. Observe the general character of the pulse, then count the number of beats for 30 seconds, multiply by two. If any deviation from normal or irregularity is noted, count for one full minute.
5. With the fingers still on the wrist, count the rise and fall of the chest or upper abdomen for 30 seconds, multiply by 2. If any irregularity or difficulty is noted, count for one full minute.
5. Record in T. P. R. book and report any abnormality.

POINTS TO EMPHASIZE
DO NOT use thumb when taking pulse beat.

V. APICAL-RADIAL PULSE

PURPOSE

To compare the pulse rate of the heart at the apex and the pulse rate in the radial artery.

EQUIPMENT

Stethoscope
Watch with second hand

PROCEDURE

1. Tell patient what you are going to do.
2. Have patient lie quietly in bed.
3. Open pajama coat to expose chest.
4. One person standing on the left side of the bed places a stethoscope over apex of heart (slightly below and to the right of the left nipple) to locate the apical heart beat.
5. Another person standing on the right side of bed locates the radial pulse; hold watch so that it can be seen by both people.
6. Using the same watch and at a signal from the person taking the apical pulse, both people count for one minute.
7. Replace pajama coat; leave patient comfortable.
8. Record in observation column on Nursing Notes (SF 510). Example: Apical 92. Radial 86.

POINTS TO EMPHASIZE

<u>Two</u> corpsmen are necessary to carry out this procedure because the two pulses must be taken at the same time to compare rates.

CARE OF EQUIPMENT

1. Wipe earpieces and diaphragm/bell of stethoscope with alcohol sponges before and after procedure.
2. Return stethoscope to proper place.

VI. TAKING BLOOD PRESSURE

PURPOSE
To determine the pressure which the blood exerts against the walls of the vessels.

EQUIPMENT
Sphygmomanometer
Stethoscope
Pencil and paper
Alcohol sponges

PROCEDURE
1. Tell patient what you are going to do.
2. Place patient in comfortable position sitting or lying down.
3. Place rubber portion of cuff over the brachial artery. Secure either by hooking or wrapping depending on the type of apparatus.
4. Clip indicator to cuff (aneroid) or place apparatus on a level surface (mercury) at about heart level. Make sure the tubing is not kinked and that it does not rub against the apparatus.
5. Locate brachial pulse at bend of elbow.
6. Place stethoscope in ears with ear pieces pointing forward.
7. Hold stethoscope in place over the brachial artery. Inflate cuff until the indicator registers 200 mm. Loosen thumb screw of valve and allow air to escape slowly.
8. Listen for the sounds. Watch the indicator. Note where the first distinct rhythmic sound is heard. This is the Systolic Pressure.
9. Continue releasing air from the cuff. Note where sound changes to dull muffled beat. This is the Diastolic Pressure.
10. Open valve completely. Release all air from cuff.
11. Remove cuff. Record reading.

POINTS TO EMPHASIZE
1. Either arm may be used in taking blood pressure, but in repeating readings, it is important to use the same arm.
2. Some departments in the hospital may define diastolic pressure as the last sound heard.
3. If unsure of reading, completely deflate cuff and repeat procedure.

CARE OF EQUIPMENT
1. Fold and replace cuff.
2. Wipe ear pieces and bell/diaphragm of stethoscope with alcohol sponge before and after procedure. Replace.

VII. RECORDING ON THE TEMPERATURE, PULSE, AND RESPIRATION FORM

PURPOSE
To keep an accurate and up-to-date record of the patient's cardinal or vital signs.

EQUIPMENT
Pen with black or blue-black ink
Standard Form 511, Temperature-Pulse-Respiration
Ruler
Addressograph plate

PROCEDURE
1. Complete identifying data in lower left corner of SF-511.
2. Fill in spaces as indicated in the heading by printing:
   Month
   Date of month.
   Hospital day.
   Postoperative or postpartum day.
   Hours T.P.R's are taken.
3. Using a small dot, record temperature and pulse in spaces corresponding vertically to hour and horizontally to scales on left side of form. Join dots of previous readings by drawing straight lines with ruler.
4. Print respiration rate in space indicated to correspond with date and hour taken.
5. Record blood pressure in space indicated to correspond with date and hour taken.
6. Record height and weight on admission in spaces provided. Repeated weight recordings are made to correspond with date and hour taken.

POINTS TO EMPHASIZE
1. For every four hour and twice a day temperature and pulse, record within dotted lines.
2. For four times a day temperature and pulse, record on dotted lines.
3. Blood pressures required more than twice a day should be graphed on a Plotting Chart (SF 512).
4. Any peculiarities of the patient that affects the temperature, pulse, or respiration, i.e.; drop in temperature due to medication; ongoing cooling procedure; and/or absences from ward, may be recorded in ..graphic column at the designated time.
5. Indicate method - if axillary or rectal is used.

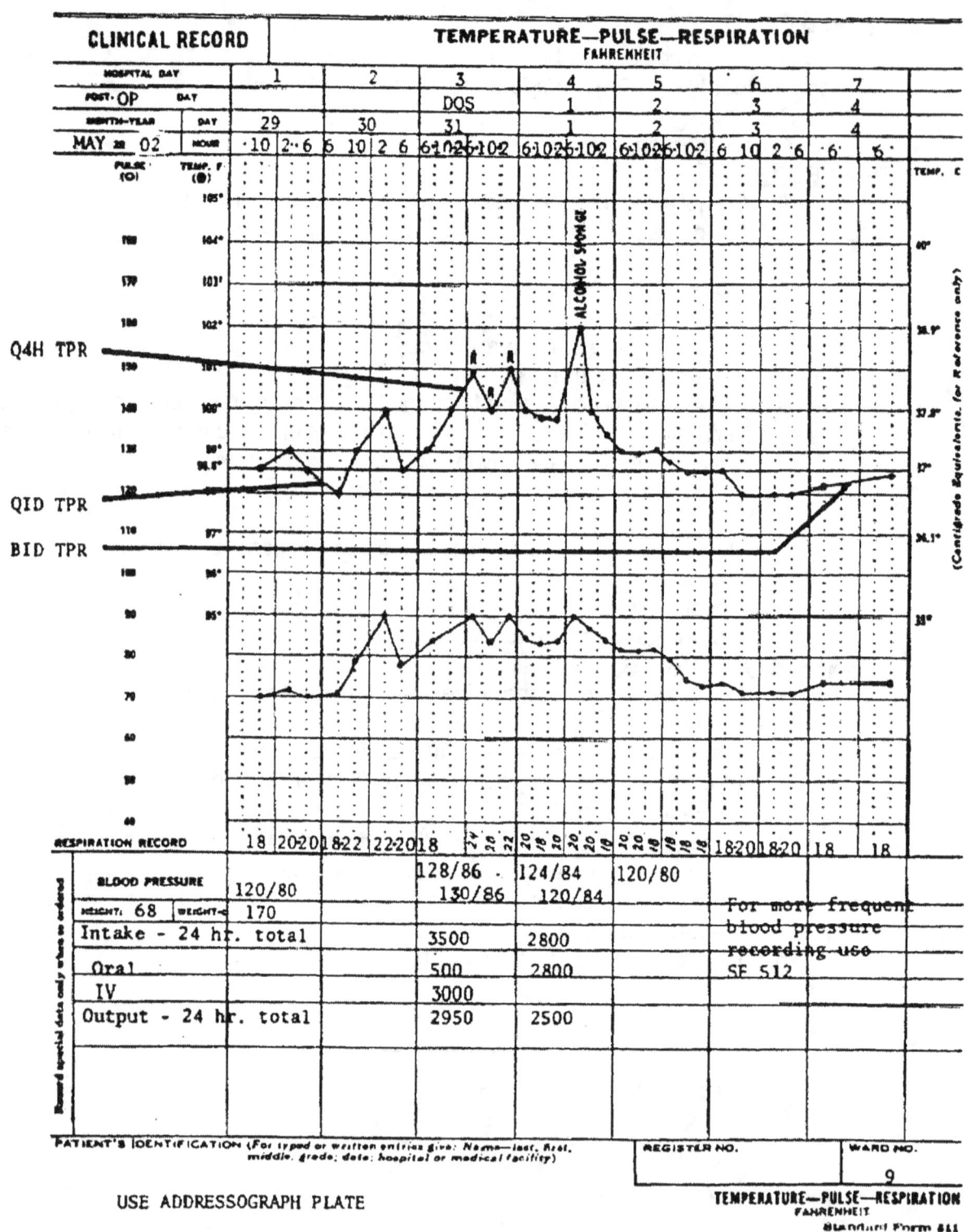

USING THE TEMPERATURE - PULSE - RESPIRATION
GRAPHIC FORM 511

All entries shall be lettered in black or blue-black ink. Ballpoint pens may be used. Each sheet should have identifying data at the foot of each page. These data should be legible, correct and complete.

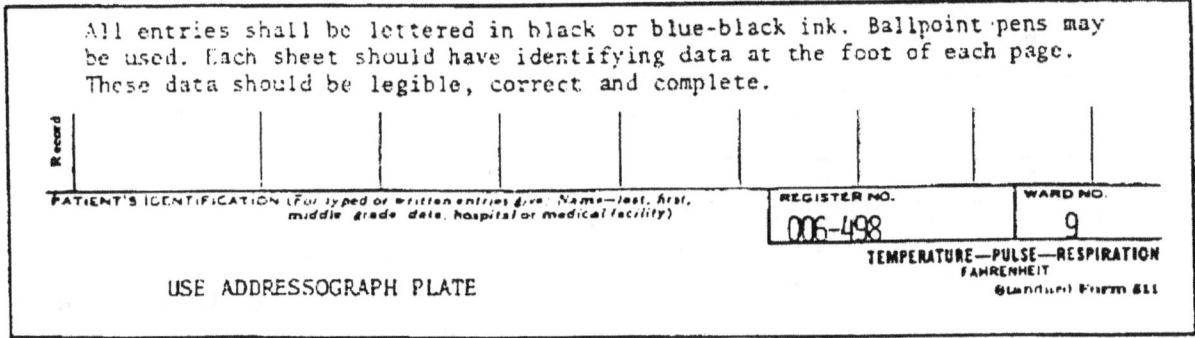

Each sheet is divided into seven major columns, one for each day of the week. The day of admission is the first hospital day.

The month, day of the month, and year appear in the spaces for that purpose. In the sample below, the patient was admitted to the hospital on May 7, 2002.

The day of operation or delivery is lettered "Operation" or "Delivery". The following day is the first postoperative or postdelivery day. For example, if the patient had surgery on his third hospital day, the chart would appear as follows:

To chart the temperature and pulse, place a dot on the graph according to the scale on the left in the vertical column that designates the correct time and date. Connect the dot of the previous recording with a solid line.

The respirations are recorded in the vertical column according to the hour.

In the sample at the left the 6 a.m. TPR was 97-72-16. The 6 p.m. TPR was 98.6-76-18.

Each day is divided into two columns, a.m. and p.m.

[Clinical record chart showing Hospital Day 1-7, Post-Op Day with DOS on day 3, then 1, 2, 3, 4; Month-Year MAY 02, Days 7-13; with a.m. and p.m. labels pointing to the two subdivisions of day 1.]

The a.m. and p.m. subdivision is further divided by two vertical dotted lines. For every four hour temperature and pulse reading, place the recordings WITHIN the dotted lines.

[Clinical record chart showing the same layout with hour markings 2-6-10 repeated for each a.m. and p.m. column; labels point to 2 a.m., 6 a.m., 10 a.m., 2 p.m., 6 p.m., 10 p.m.]

Twice a day temperature and pulse recordings are placed WITHIN the dotted lines in the center of the a.m. and p.m. column.

[Clinical record chart with hour markings "·6·" in each column; labels point to 6 a.m. and 6 p.m.]

For four-times-a-day readings, place the recordings ON the dotted lines.

[Clinical record chart with hour markings 6 10 2 6 repeated; labels point to 6 a.m., 10 a.m., 2 p.m., 6 p.m.]

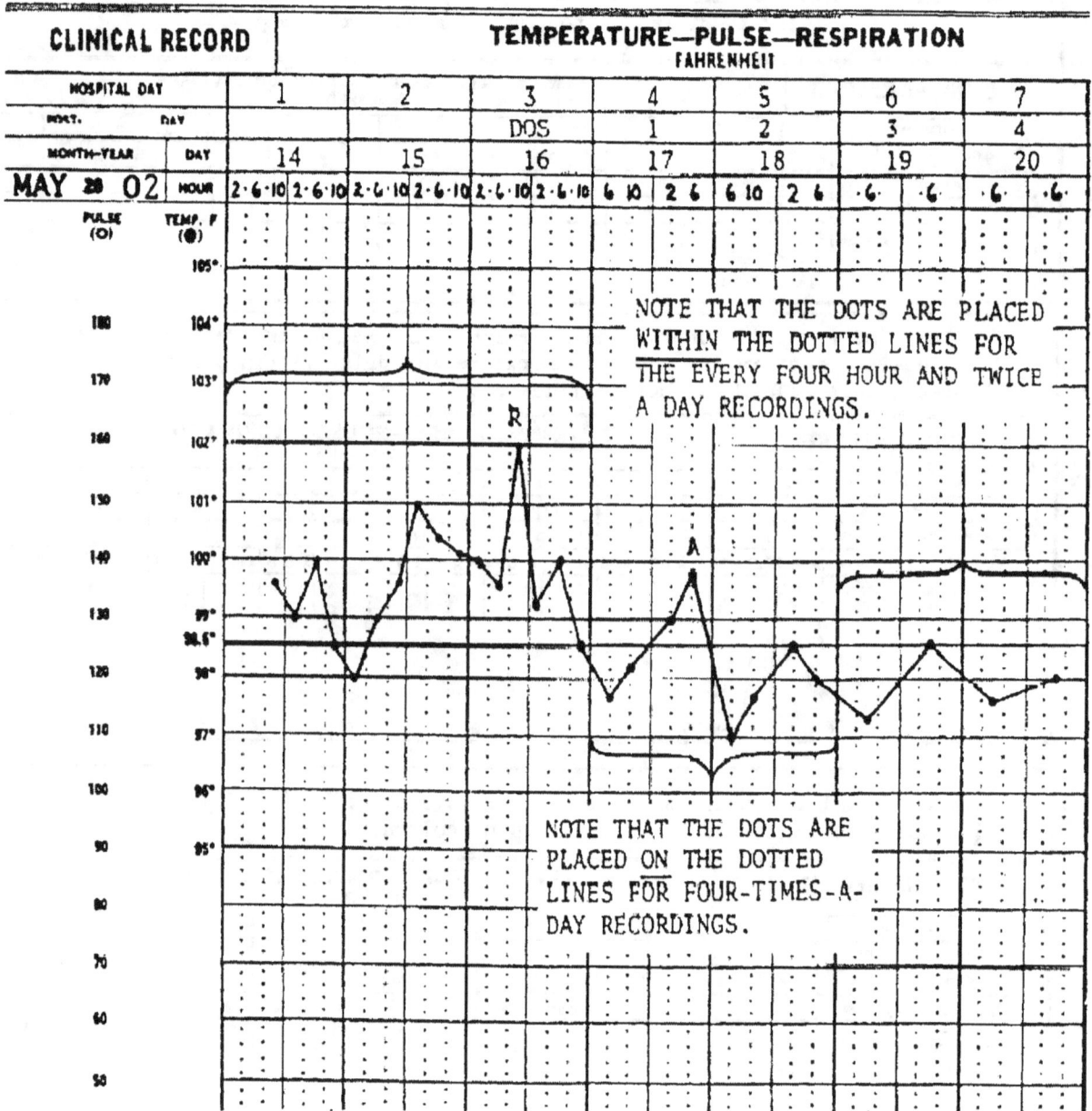

If a temperature is taken by rectum, place an "R" (for rectal) above the dot on the graph.
If a temperature is taken by axilla, place an "A" (for axillary) above the dot on the graph.

VIII. RECORDING ON PLOTTING CHART

PURPOSE

To keep an accurate, visible record of repeated observations of intake-output, weight, blood pressure, etc.

EQUIPMENT

Pen with, black or blue-black ink
Standard Form 512, Plotting Chart
Ruler

PROCEDURE

1. Complete identifying data in lower left corner of chart. (Page 25)
2. Print date and purpose in upper left corner.
3. Calibrate measurements along vertical portion of graph:
    Start scale at bottom working toward top at a definite and uniform rate of progression, as 0-10-20.30.
    Label scale at top to show unit of measure as cc. , lbs. , or mm.
4. Note date time intervals of measure along top horizontal portion of graph.
5. Show meaning of symbols used in a key to the side of graph.

Note: Red pencil may be ued when filling in bar graphs.

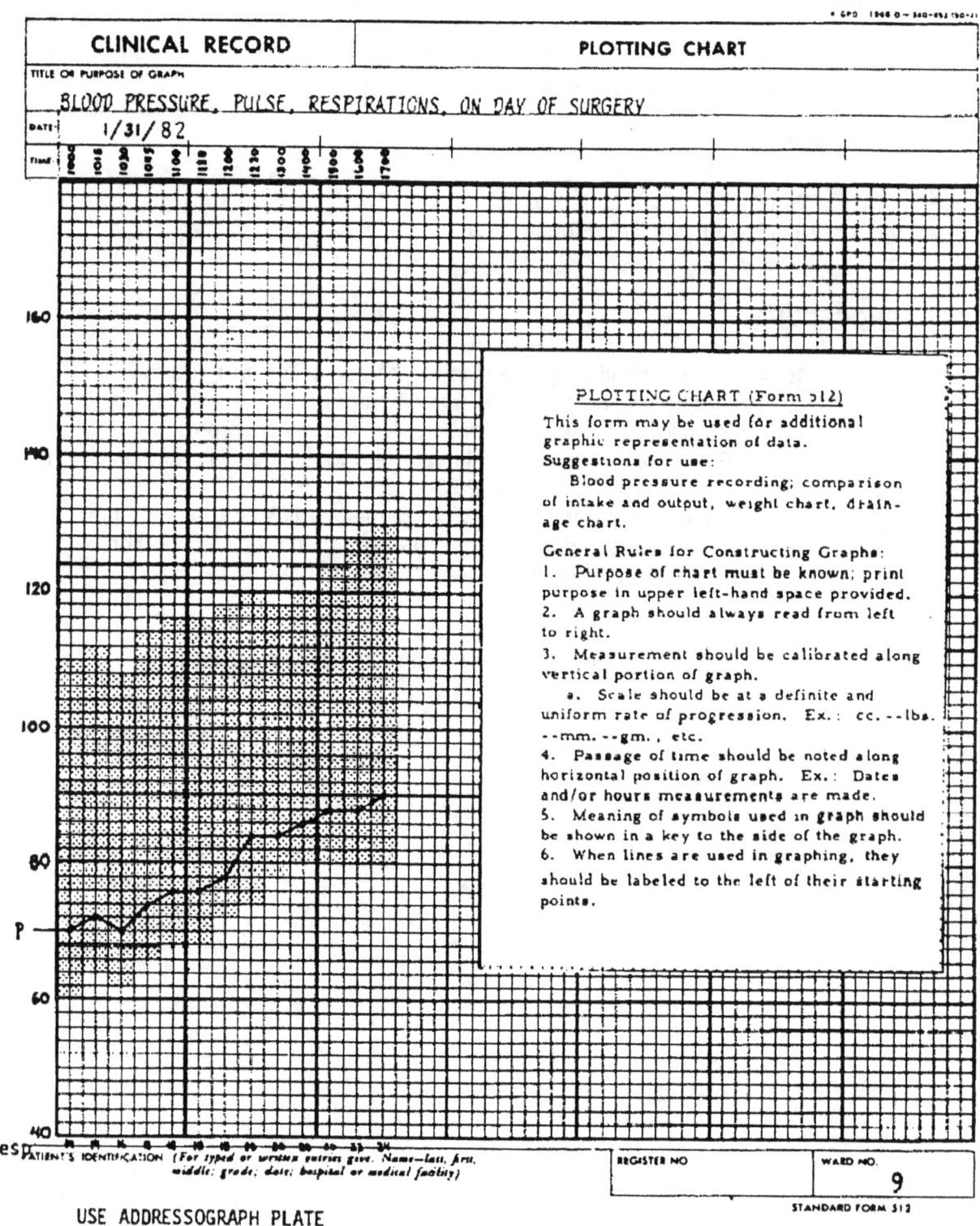